Finding Myself in
AVIATION

Mary S. Build

To my daughters, Anna and Lisa,
whose curiosity introduced me to aviation.

TABLE OF CONTENTS

INTRODUCTION

At the age of 76, I decided it was time to hang up my wings, because it was better to stop when I was flying very well instead of waiting for something bad to happen.

I found that when I flew that last year, I kept watching to see when I would make a mistake. It didn't make sense to me to end my love of flying with an accident. However, my soul misses the sky.

What I miss most is floating above the ice-covered lakes and ponds in Maine, lifting one wing and then the other to wave. Ice fishermen, snowmobilers, and snowshoers all looked up at the humming sound above them and waved back. I smiled every time.

What a joy it was to land on the ice at Alton Bay on Lake Winnipesaukee and have near strangers come up to me as I got out of the plane and greet me by name. It was thrilling, but I never knew how so many people knew me.

Perhaps my time volunteering for Aviation Career Education (ACE) Camps was part of it. The past six years, I've flown to Laconia, New Hampshire, landed on the runway, and joined the other volunteers to introduce interested young men and women to a variety of roles in aviation. I always arrived on my amphibious floats, taxied to the south side of the field, around a building, and parked beside the cars in the parking lot. I did this because I could—and it felt comfortable to do something out of the ordinary.

I miss the camaraderie of my pilot friends who enjoyed the adventures of flying on skis, landing on Moosehead Lake for breakfast, which always turned into lunch, and then flying further northeast to Chesuncook Lake. There we were taken to the Lake House in a snowmobile-drawn trailer towed by a teenager. We hopped on and held on for dear life, but it saved us the trek through three feet of snow so we could enjoy warm homemade pie and delicious hot coffee.

Leaving Chesuncook, enjoying the colorful late-afternoon sky, we flew southwest to Rangeley, over the frozen lakes, down through the mountains, and back home. I would land on our snow-covered field and taxi back to the heated hangar. I took the bulk of the snow off the skis outside the hangar and used an aviation tug to tow my plane back in where I could finish cleaning it up for the next flight.

I enjoyed working around the plane and cleaning it off after every flight just as much as flying each season: bugs in the summer and snow in the winter.

Those years have gone by faster than I wanted, but I keep the memories by writing about my love of flying. I have been fortunate to have so many rewarding experiences to hold onto, and I love sharing them with others.

Flying changed my life in many ways. I had found a career that was a constant challenge to learn more and that helped me to be more confident in knowing I could understand something at a higher level than office work. The best part of aviation was sharing my love for it with others.

I discovered I was a good instructor. When I was in high school, the thought of being a teacher was at the bottom of my list of desired occupations. All I could see was standing in front of a class of kids who didn't want to be there. When I was teaching flying, my students were all in and gave me more satisfaction than I could possibly imagine.

I never expected that surviving an overturned seaplane and almost drowning would be a turning point in my original desire to be a seaplane charter pilot before I even had a pilot's license. Or that those clouds dropping down on me in the middle of mountainous terrain on one of my trips to Alaska would make me a stronger person.

The most important thing I learned was that I was much happier and successful when I found something I wanted to do—and not because someone else thought it was what I *should* do. Once I launched into aviation, other members of the aviation community gave me the support and direction I could only have dreamed of.

I hope you'll enjoy hearing about my adventures as much as I had living them.

—*Mary Build*
January 2022

30 SUMMER STREET

Cohasset, Massachusetts
1944–1953

When I think of flying, the first thing that comes to mind is freedom. Freedom to roam east or west. Freedom to investigate whether there is still ice on the ponds in the spring, or to see if snowmobiles have been on the lakes in the winter.

When I look down from above, I wonder what it's like living in some of the smaller homes. Then, would there be too much room in the larger ones? What are the people like who are living there? Some homes are tucked away in the side of a hill where they cannot be seen from the road. Do the people in those isolated spots want to be left alone, or are they artists who need peace and quiet to accomplish their creations? Don't they need a view? I know I would.

The larger fields are a lovely bright green in the spring, and their crops wave in the wind during the summer. I can distinguish sod farms by the straight rows of neatly mowed grass and the light-brown earth strips where the sod was removed. Where is the sod going? Did someone just build a new house, or is it going to resurface the baseball field in Fenway Park?

Life has not always been like that. I've always been curious, but never felt free. During my younger years, until I was eight, I roamed around town to stay out of the way. Roamed where I wanted and hoped someone would talk to me.

Mrs. Freeman opened the door and said, "Hello. What's your name?"

"Mary Shyne," I replied with a broad smile across my face.

"Hello, dear. Would you like to come in?"

"Yes, please."

"I was just going to collect some eggs from the henhouse. Would you like to come along?"

"Oh, yes." Nothing like a good adventure. I had no idea where eggs came from.

We brought the eggs that were left in the little straw nests back into the kitchen and I sat down to see what was going to happen next.

"What's this?" I asked as I took a big sniff and dropped the pepper as if it was going to make me sneeze again.

"That was pepper, dear," she giggled as her robust tummy bounced up and down.

I observed the watchmaker in the jewelry store and the pharmacist counting pills in the pharmacy. On each occasion, a tall stool was put next to them for me to sit on so I was up high enough to see what was being done. Theresa, who lived across the street, taught me how to play Crazy Eights and ping-pong. I felt happy being in such a friendly neighborhood. I didn't want to go home.

I was sad at home most of the time. The youngest of six with a seven-year gap between me and my next oldest sibling put me in the position to be the scapegoat in the family. My four older brothers were used to teasing each other, so when I came along, I eventually became a new target. It was like growing up as an only child with many overseeing, taking care of, loving, but never including me in their lives. When they went out with their friends, I never understood why I couldn't go with them. They were friends with each other. Decisions were discussed and made by them, and I was told what my part was. I was never included in the decision-making process itself.

One day when I was four, everyone else was in school. I wandered into the kitchen and found my mother busy at the counter making something.

"Can I help?"

"Sure you can," she said as she placed a stool on the floor that was the one I usually stood on so I could reach the sink to brush my teeth.

"Can I stir?"

"Yes, but you must stir like this," she explained as she moved the spoon around in a clockwise direction.

"Why do I have to do it that way?"

"To mix the ingredients together," she said.

"Will it come apart if I do it the other way?"

"Yes, it will."

I investigated the contents in the bowl and wondered if it would come undone, so I went the other way, counterclockwise, to find out. As a four-year-old, I didn't see anything wrong with that.

"I told you to do it this way," she said angrily as she grabbed my hand and went in the direction she wanted me to stir.

"Now go outdoors and play. Go visit Theresa," she said sternly, grabbing the spoon from my hand.

I spent more time with Theresa, watching her bake, licking the spoon, and helping her by drying dishes. I neatly piled them on the metal kitchen table. She always found four-leaf clovers and had them in a little jar of water over the sink. I looked and looked for them, but never found one myself.

Theresa never seemed to tire of me hanging around. We spent what seemed like hours playing ping-pong in the basement. I don't ever remember anyone playing with me at home—at least before I was eight, anyway.

Something was missing at home.

I remember crying one day at home. I was hurting and honestly thought no one loved me. I could not stop crying. With tears and a broken heart, I told my mother how sad I was. My chest felt tight, as if someone was pressing on it.

"Don't be ridiculous," she said. "You have four brothers who love you."

I wanted her to stop working, sit down, and hold me. Right then. I wanted to hear her say, "Oh, no. I love you." I wanted her to kiss my forehead like she did before I went to sleep at night. I wanted her to wipe away my tears. I wanted to hear "I love you" while she comforted me. I never heard her say that. Ever. As I was sobbing, she stood there looking down at me and smiling. Why was she thinking this was funny?

Another response when I cried was, "Stop your crying or I'll give you something to cry about!"

One day I came home crying with a scraped knee after falling off a granite curb on the sidewalk.

"I told you not to walk on the edge of the sidewalk!"

I cried even harder, because I never remembered her telling me that. I wouldn't have done it if she had. Why would she tell me not to walk on the curb anyway? She never took me for a walk.

The days of feeling as if I didn't belong, or that I was in the way, were depressing. What hurt the most was when my mother would dismiss me with a surly flip of her hand and a look of disgust on her face. I didn't feel like a bad kid. I didn't intentionally do anything wrong. When I did, I had bruises big enough on my backside to make the doctor question me.

"How did you get these?" I made up some excuse because I didn't know how to explain. How could I admit they were from the one person I expected to protect me, but who never did? After that visit to the doctor, my mother never hit me again.

Mother seemed to be suspicious of every move I made. It was confusing and painful to not be trusted. I remember losing one of my shoes when I was six. How could that possibly happen in small living quarters on one side of a duplex? I never figured it out. I could not find that lost shoe anywhere. I prayed to St. Anthony as hard as I could to help me. Being the patron saint of lost things, surely he could help me find my shoe to stop my mother from being so mad at me. He didn't help. I had never asked for help before, so I was a little unsure of the validity of his strength.

Mother said, "You lost that shoe on purpose. You never liked them, so you've hidden that one somewhere. Now find it." I never did. I didn't hide it, either.

The day I received First Communion, I couldn't get home fast enough to get out of that uncomfortable white dress and silly veil. I was in my comfy T-shirt and Wrangler boy jeans, and asked my friend Judy if she wanted to come play with me. She was still in her white clothes from our special day in church, but that didn't matter.

On one of my latest adventures, I had found little brooks running through the marsh behind our house, and I loved jumping over them. Judy wasn't as agile as I, and she missed the other bank. Her white shoes and socks were about four inches into the mud, and I had to help her get unstuck. That created a bit of tugging and pulling, which caused the pretty white dress to get some muddy smears on the front. I came home with her and thought nothing of the situation. A little soap and water would fix her right up.

Before I knew what was going to happen, Mother came tearing into the living room and said, "You are a naughty little girl, taking Judy with you and letting her get all muddy."

I couldn't believe that such an innocent activity could be twisted like that.

"I didn't do that on purpose."

"Oh yes you did," she stated emphatically.

My brother Jim, who was 13 at the time, used to whittle pieces of wood, carving beautiful animals. I tried that skill, but it evaded me. However, I did like throwing the jackknife and having it land blade down into the ground. I practiced it every day and was fascinated that it always ended up stuck with the blade where it was supposed to be. One day, Nancy, who was another more fragile friend, came over to see if I wanted to play. I instinctively knew she would be afraid of the knife and wouldn't be impressed with my throwing skills. I hid it behind my back to keep the evidence out of sight until I could put it away. Mother called me into the house. I never hesitated a minute when she called. I was scared to death of her.

"That is a terrible thing you were going to do," she said sternly.

"What?"

"You were going to hurt Nancy with that knife. Let me have that right now."

"I wasn't going to do that."

"Oh yes you were! You've picked that up from watching television and you are not to watch it again for a week."

Not sure how Howdy Doody could have affected me like that. I never saw him use knives. That was the only show I ever watched on our new TV.

I wished I lived somewhere else and tried for years to find another mother to be with.

Mother was adamant we all have good manners. One day I was brought into the living room and ordered to sit down on the couch.

"Now, when you meet someone, you shake their hand firmly and look them in the eyes. They will say, 'Hi, Mary, how are you?' You are to answer, 'Very well, thank you. How are you?'"

Again and again we practiced until I had it down.

Family dynamics are intricate in many ways. Affection and being unwelcome came at the same time and at different levels for me. The order of my siblings was Frank, John, Kevin, Bernadette and Jim. The first five were born in six years. My brother Frank was 13 when I was born, and John was 12. Mother often reminded me that John used to take care of my two a.m. feedings when I came home from the hospital. We had a bond right from the start. He was the one who spent time with me. That's what I wanted...I craved attention. Frank and John used to tease me, but at least it was at the level of kindness. Not a lot of fun to be on the receiving end, but I knew they loved me.

When my brothers heard I had been put through the "How do you do" drill, they started in on me. I thought they were helping me practice.

John said, "Hi, Mary, how are you?"

"Very well, thank you. How are you?"

He repeated, "Very well, thank you. How are you?"

"Very well, thank you. How are you?"

After five or six times, I was thoroughly confused. The boys thought it was hysterical. Today, I can't remember a single person's name after meeting them due to making sure I say everything just right. I'm sure there must be other reasons, but I always focus on being as polite as I can.

I remember Frank, who was then 17 and I was four, playing an instrumental song on the record player in the living room. We didn't have a television then, and I was intent on his description.

He said, "See if you can hear in the music how the Sorcerer is going down the stairs into the flooded cellar." He was playing Walt Disney's *Fantasia*.

"Can you hear the danger?" I was fascinated that he could derive that from listening to music. That experience sparked a love for music in me and an appreciation of Frank's intelligence.

When it was John's turn to care for me, he would take me by the hand and walk to the "Cove" so I could spend some of my 25¢ allowance on penny candy. It was a long way for my little legs, but really only two-tenths of a mile. We were expected to put part of our allowance in the savings bank, give some to the church, and we could spend a reasonable amount on what we wanted.

John was incredibly patient. The Cove was where several streets came together around the boat-filled harbor with many working lobster boats and elegant Chris-Craft mahogany pleasure boats. I loved going down there. That's where all the activity was—with a gas station, a restaurant, and a little general store that had eye-level candy for sale.

Another day, John gave me a ride in the rumble seat of a car. We didn't own a car, so I don't know where this one came from, but I felt free as a bird with the wind blowing through my hair and against my face. I felt so special that he had asked me to go for a ride. I loved going to the drugstore when he was working behind the soda fountain. He always made me a single-scoop ice cream, either chocolate, lemon sherbet, chocolate chip, or vanilla—whatever was the favorite of the week. I was so proud I had a brother who worked there and was excited to see me come in the door.

Kevin was only ten when I arrived on the scene, and he made a go-cart for me when I was very little. I was ecstatic thinking I could drive around in my own vehicle under my own power. The day I was brought outside to try it, he was on the top of the list of favorite brothers.

When Frank and John were getting ready to go to college, they each gave me a T-shirt. One was white with a Notre Dame emblem, and one had Boston College emblazoned across it. I put on the Boston College one, since John was my favorite, and that was his college of choice. I pranced down the stairs just as proud as I could be.

Frank met me at the bottom and said, "Hey, I thought I was your favorite brother!" Oh brother, I was in trouble. I didn't want to hurt his feelings, so I ran back upstairs and put on the Notre Dame shirt. Again, I flew down the stairs to prove my loyalty and John met me at the bottom.

"Hey, I thought I was your favorite brother!" Oh no. What a dilemma. I went back up and put them both on. I was not going to hurt either one of these guys. Coming down the next time, both were at the bottom and the discussion ensued as to which one was on top. I couldn't win and burst into tears. They had no idea how important it was to me that they knew I loved them. They thought it was funny and tried to comfort me, but I was devastated. I really did love both of them and I just hoped they knew it, for I was out of options.

In the corner of the dining room beside the telephone table was a huge whiskey bottle almost as tall as I was. We were all directed to put our money into the bottle to save for "the boys' college education," Mother used to say.

Bernadette was eight when I was born, and like anything else for me, when something is painful or sad, I remember it more than the fun times. While Mother was punishing her to pay for her most recent "crime," Bernadette refused to cry. More than likely it wasn't anything serious. It could have been as simple as talking back to Mother, but Mother needed help and there were no maids to do it for her. Talking back was never acceptable, but the punishment was always far worse than the crime. Poor Bernadette would iron for hours, and I felt so sorry for her. However, I had to keep my distance, because I didn't want to get into trouble for feeling sorry for her.

The ironing board was set up in the dining room and she had to iron my brothers' work uniforms. They wore heavy white starched chef's attire that had to be washed, starched, and ironed every day.

Frank and John put themselves through college working at an expensive restaurant down at the harbor that catered to summer residents. Frank worked on the charcoal broiler in the dining room and John on the salad bar, with Bernadette helping him. Kevin's job was preparing food in the kitchen, and my youngest brother, Jim, parked cars as a valet.

Bernadette never said an unkind word to me even though she was burdened with my care on frequent occasions. We shared a bed that was a couch during the day and a pull-out bed at night.

One day, she told Mother she was going to babysit for a neighbor's child who was a year older than I.

"That's fine, but if you can take care of him, you have to take Mary with you."

I wanted to be her friend, not her baggage. I didn't want to go but had no choice.

Another day, my sister was going to ride her bike to the beach with her friends.

"That's a nice idea, but Mary has to go with you. I'm busy today." I only had little legs at age seven and couldn't keep up with her. She had to keep stopping for me to catch up. I felt terrible for holding her up and that she had to take me with her.

To top it all off, Bernadette was punished again because we both got terrible sunburns and ended up with sunstroke. We were secluded in the den/our bedroom in the dark for days after getting too much sun. We saw big circles around any light, proving that our eyes were also damaged. When we recovered, Bernadette was forced to iron again for hours. Punishment in the summer for Bernadette was ironing, and during the winter it was cleaning the silver. She infuriated Mother when she sang while she worked.

Jim was the baby in the family for seven years before my arrival. I never felt any affection from him—and I would do anything to get it. I wanted him to like me the way he liked my other siblings. He took me aside one day and told me how I could help Frank, our neighbor across the street, because he was lonely.

I was drawn to our neighbor Frank, not to be confused with my brother Frank. He let me tighten and loosen the vise in his neatly arranged garage. I was impressed with his tools hanging on the white painted peg board on the back wall of the garage. Each tool was outlined with black paint as it hung there.

"A place for everything and everything in its place," he said.

We went to the dump together in his ugly green car to get parts for a footrest we were going to make together. We found springs and odd pieces of wood lying around the smelly dump as we dug through the trash that wasn't burning. When the stool was finished, he told me to turn it over, and my name was on the bottom in big block letters: MARY. He must really care about me, I thought.

I was also impressed that he had built their brick house and garage. There also was a little white and green wooden building down in the backyard that he had built.

He always smelled like ale. Theresa always had a nice cold one for him as soon as he got home from work. He also had a funny metal smell. I guessed that came from the shipyard where he worked.

Frank was quite an artist and painted beautiful murals in the basement of the house. The scene was a neat mahogany-walled stable with black bars on the upper part of the stall. I particularly liked the way a plaid horse blanket was hanging on the side of the stall. It was on a wooden bar suspended by small chains on either end. Tethered to the cross-ties was a handsome dark-brown stallion with large expressive eyes. Frank pointed out the specific male parts of a stallion standing in the barn.

He was setting me up in an invisible web of deceit: convinced me I was needed, loved, having me traipse around after him, guaranteed that everyone would be mad at me if I told what we did. Theresa would especially be mad at me. I couldn't bear to lose her, so I swore to secrecy.

My brother Jim said, "Theresa and Frank don't even share the same bedroom." This was unheard of, because my parents shared their bed in a lovely bedroom, and I couldn't imagine it any other way. I wanted to help Frank because he spent so much time with me. If Jimmy said it was okay, then it must be. I had no idea what kind of commitment this was going to be, but I understood what feeling lonely was like. I found out 40 years later that Jim had been abused by Frank, too.

Theresa preserved vegetables from the garden, and they were kept in the cold-storage room in the cellar. My friends and I played hide-and-seek, and Frank was with me in that chilly dark room holding me against him. It felt strange, because no one ever held me that way, but it was special to be the only one Frank chose to be with him hiding in the dark. Going to the dump, working on the footstool together, and helping pick beans in the garden with Frank was fun. He made me feel superior, because I was filling a need for him. The things that went on in the little white cabin in the backyard were not something a little girl of four and five years old should be introduced to. Unfortunately, it created feelings of sexual desire in me. I shouldn't have grown up so fast. But at the time, I felt it was normal and exciting.

That behavior came in dribs and drabs but continued until I was eight. It became a lifelong lesson about helping some poor needy man that I was sure I could help at some level. If they were married and unhappy, they were perfect for me to help. It took years to get over that compulsion.

The insidious way pedophiles continue to prey on other children is because it is passed on by the abused. I was encouraged to bring my neighborhood friends to Frank and Theresa's house. I never encouraged them to do anything wrong. I told them we could play ping-pong and Crazy Eights, and enjoy the wooden swing in the backyard. I found out decades later in therapy that when I brought other children into the pedophile's reach, it was a self-defense mechanism to take the pressure off me. In a sick and distorted way, I was jealous when my friends got too much attention. I wanted it all, but I didn't want it at all. What a confusing way to start out in life.

In a different neighbor's backyard, I was introducing another child to something when his mother informed me that it was not acceptable.

"If you don't go and tell your mother what you are doing, I will," she said angrily.

Telling Mother what was going on with the neighbor Frank, and that other kids in the neighborhood were involved, was a frightening decision for me to make, but at the same time, a relief. I wouldn't have to go through that anymore.

I told her that Jim had sent me over there and told me to "help" Frank. Her response was, "Let me ask your brother."

She came back to me a day later saying, "Jim said no such thing every happened."

Why would she believe him and not me? Her not believing me was devastating. How could a child make up something like that unless exposed to it? It's not possible. I never confided in her again, and the abuse continued.

One day, when roaming around town as my mother assumed I was in the neighborhood, I stopped in at St. Anthony's Church. I walked right up to where the votive candles were on the right side of the altar. I knew that lighting a candle was for saying a special prayer, and I was supposed to pay a quarter to do so. I didn't have a quarter to put in the little black box, but it didn't matter. I was in desperate need. I took one of the long wooden matches, held it over the flame of one of the lighted candles and lit my own candle. I blew out the match, laid it down on the little black shelf and knelt on the kneeler.

"Please, dear God, help me to not grow up like my mother." I included a Hail Mary and an Our Father to convince God I was serious.

Unfortunately, being brought up like that didn't help me to be the person I felt deep down inside that I should be. I was angry, didn't work hard in school, and didn't choose healthy relationships. I went to nursing school, hated it, and dropped out. I met Tony, my first husband, who was ten years older than I, and thought I would finally be happy. All I really did was get right back into being treated the way I'd been when I was growing up: feeling trapped.

FREEDOM

When I was 23, I lived in a lovely New England cape-style home set back from the road. It was the last house on a dead-end street. The landscaping had been professionally done 25 years before with well-maintained shrubs that I enjoyed trimming and shaping. I loved clipping the yews to keep them manageable but looking natural. The house stood on the top of a bank overlooking the North River in Hanover, Massachusetts. The garage was a car's length from the road with a stone wall running along the left side and a Japanese quince next to the side door on the right that led to a winding walkway to the house. Looking to the right on the way to the back door while walking down that path, there was an apple tree, and beyond that, six blueberry bushes that gave us fruit all year. Closer to the road were two very tall spruce trees inside the neatly trimmed privet hedge. All this looked terrific from the outside.

In the house there were freshly refurbished hardwood floors, braided rugs, and new furniture. The best part of the house was the view from the dining room and living room bay windows, allowing me to see 180 degrees outside and down to the river. I was always up early and enjoyed a peaceful few minutes each morning gazing at the river, which was constantly moving. There was a fish ladder for spawning salmon upriver. In the spring, thousands of newly hatched babies popped up and down on their way to the ocean. Occasionally, a Canada goose would float by. I should have been very happy in this environment.

The kitchen was the room where I spent most of my time. The dark-green 25-year-old linoleum tiles were cracked and curling, while the rubbish was in the only available spot under the counter, right beside the stove and next to the small round table where we ate all our meals. I wanted this room finished. I didn't think there was a problem with money, since Tony owned a restaurant, owned a horse that was stabled nearby, and drove a Cadillac.

One afternoon in June, Tony arrived home with a bright-red 18' Old Town Canoe with sponsons (increased floatation on the sides), expecting me to be thrilled. I was not. He and our neighbor took the cellophane-wrapped canoe out of the back of a borrowed pickup truck and set it on the ground. I had no part in the decision making of this purchase and felt the flow of money was going in the wrong direction. I didn't feel right expressing my feelings in front of our neighbor, but I was later told I showed no appreciation and that the neighbor was disappointed in my reaction. I felt I was damned if I had said anything and damned if I hadn't.

There was not much to do on a dead-end street that was closed off by a highway at the end of the road. I didn't have a car and felt trapped. Worse than that, I had no idea where I would go if I had one. I was bored and frustrated not knowing how to be a good mother.

All I could do with my three-year-old child was introduce her to all the things I loved. I took her to the barn to see her dad's horse, and sometimes riding with me as she sat in front of me on the horse.

The experience I'd had as a child had left a poor example of how to be a good mother. My mother never spent time like that with me.

Looking back, it's clear I was suffering from depression, but I had no idea of that at the time. I only knew I was painfully sad and lonely. I wanted a husband to stand beside me, not better than or lesser than me. I wanted a partner to share in making decisions, to love and be loved. I didn't have that. With a three-year-old child, I had no idea that I might have any other option than to stay and put up with life the best I could. Where would I go?

One day, I bundled my daughter Anna up in a bright orange life jacket that she didn't want to wear. I told her it was a boat coat and that she needed to wear it when going for a ride. She liked that idea, and we headed for the canoe to try it out. I had grown up on the water and learned to row when I was five. I had swimming lessons every year, always progressing ahead of everyone else in my class. I then took sailing lessons when I was 13. I loved being on the water more than any sport I ever played.

The canoe had just been lying on the grass down by the river. I had been stubborn about not having anything to say about its purchase, so I hadn't used it. But that day, something was different. The tide was going out, and my intention was to glide along downstream with the current and then come back when it turned. Being 14 miles upriver, the change of tide was three hours behind where it was on the ocean, so I easily calculated how long our trip would be.

Anna sat in front of me as I knelt on the bottom of the canoe, leaning back against the stern seat. It felt too top-heavy when I sat on the seat. I didn't know how to paddle a canoe, but it came naturally to me. I didn't know the J stroke at that time, but managed nicely moving the paddle from side to side to keep us in a straight line as we slowly moved along with the current. I felt relaxed and in my element on the water and wished I could always feel that joy.

The water was cool to the touch as I reached my hand over the side, my fingers sliding along, causing a small ripple behind as it spread out just as the wake of the canoe was doing. Both were barely visible because I was going so slow.

Anna did the same thing as she leaned over the side, and we silently enjoyed the experience. At first, I was afraid she would fall overboard, but I wanted to let her explore and not be frightened in a boat. She had a life jacket on that fit properly, and I was right there to grab her if necessary. We rounded a rather large rock and slid under an old arched stone bridge. There were vines covering a good part of the weathered sides of the bridge and hanging down from the top.

On the other side of the bridge, in front of a big three-story farmhouse with an attached barn, there was something I had never seen before: a shiny silver plane on pontoons up on the slightly sloped marshy embankment. I wondered how it had gotten there. How did someone get it that far from the water? (It never occurred to me at the time that it was put there when the river was high.) Not knowing anything about airplanes, or ones that could fly on and off the water, no more thought went into this unexpected sight.

With the slight rocking of the boat and the warm sun on her back, Anna was soon stretched out on the floor sound asleep using a red square floatation cushion as a pillow. I felt as peaceful as the chirping birds that were settling on top of the developing cattails along the banks. I had been paddling for about half an hour when the current started to change. For a short period of time, we were motionless as I absorbed the beauty of the surrounding sights and sounds.

I heard the roar of an engine coming and assumed it must be the floatplane. I was concerned the pilot wouldn't be able to see our little red canoe, so I headed to the side next to the muddy bank and turned to watch the plane come around the corner. The noise came closer and closer, and the plane finally appeared. I was down low and looking up at it, and it seemed much larger than I'd expected. I was convinced the pilot couldn't see us, so I tucked into a bend away from what I thought would be his path. Anna woke up with the sound and looked around, as curious as I. She wasn't frightened. This was another new experience for her, too.

The plane continued coming toward us without affecting me physically, but emotionally I was delighted to be there to enjoy the experience. The canoe gently rolled back and forth with the resulting wake of the plane harmlessly passing. It continued on to a straight portion of the river. The engine roared, and after a short time, the plane lifted off the narrow waterway with a trail of water spraying behind it, along with a gentle breeze that floated over us from the whirling propeller.

Never in my wildest dreams could I imagine such freedom. I just sat there in awe of someone being able to fly a plane from their backyard, taking off and going wherever they wanted to go. I couldn't imagine how I could do something like that. It never entered my mind.

I didn't have any goals at the time other than being the best mother I could be. I'd married at 19 and missed a chunk of growing up by marrying so young. I was trying to do my best, but I needed to do something else. Go where, or do what, I had no idea. I was convinced I had lost my opportunity to go to school or to choose a career.

Unfortunately, that state of depression put me in the vulnerable position of being easily criticized by my husband and accepting that I was not talented in any way. If I was asked to help with anything, it was a menial job such as pulling nails from boards so they could be used again as he sat in his office making decisions for his restaurant. I had been asked to do something belittling, but I did it. Did I really think that little of myself? I just seemed to float along in life the way I was doing in the canoe.

Seeing the freedom that pilot experienced in his plane had planted a seed, but it seemed unreachable to me. I didn't know how to plant a garden like that. I didn't see it as an opportunity for me. I lacked the confidence it required to even think about becoming a pilot.

We floated back home with the knowledge that I had to do something constructive with my life. I felt more at home on the water and being part of an adventure than I did in my house. And just like my house, everything looked good on the outside, but inside my needs were not being met. I needed to make a change.

I finally reached out to a psychiatrist for help when I was 30, and it felt as though I was reaching out my arms to be pulled from a very dark hole I had fallen into a long time ago. It took years, three therapists, and learning to fly to make me whole.

COLOR OF MY PARACHUTE

After taking a scenic flight from an airport in Marshfield, Massachusetts, in August of 1975 to celebrate Anna's tenth birthday, I never thought about being a pilot, or even going to the airport again. I thought people who owned airplanes were rich or needed a plane to travel for business. I didn't fit into either of those situations and felt as if I didn't belong.

In October that same year, I joined my daughter Lisa for a scenic seaplane ride to celebrate her fifth birthday. Going to the water to fly was a different story. I loved that idea. There was something about the adventure, freedom, and peacefulness the experience promised that resonated with me. From the moment I walked down the ramp to board the plane, I was enthralled. We were taking an airplane ride from water.

I was 30 at the time, and it reminded me of the first time I'd seen a plane taking off from the North River seven years before and sensing the freedom the pilot must have felt. I couldn't imagine the thrill of piloting a seaplane. It never occurred to me that I might be capable of that. However, after working in an office and feeling more confident of myself, I had become open to something new and adventurous.

We climbed into the plane on Monponsett Pond in Halifax, Massachusetts, and Peter, our pilot, adjusted our seat belts. Lisa sat in the front with him and I sat in the back. He pushed the plane away from the dock, then hopped in while pushing in knobs and flipping switches to start the plane.

We glided to the furthest end of the lake with the engine roaring in my ears. He turned the plane around facing the shoreline that had the lowest trees and added full power. I could feel myself being pushed back in the seat from the forward motion. Water was splashing up from the floats beside my window, and in a short distance, we lifted off the water.

Thrilling! I looked ahead and saw the trees at the end of the pond, but we glided over those and climbed into the air. I was in love with that experience.

We flew a short distance over to our house on the North River in Hanover, then followed the river to the mouth in Humarock, where it merged into the ocean. During the summer, we spent a great deal of time as a family on the North River. We enjoyed lunch at the mouth of the river, which is called "The Spit." While flying over that area, I was reminded of so many joyful memories and especially loved the aerial view.

It was a crystal-clear day, and we could see forever in all directions from Boston to Provincetown on Cape Cod. I knew where we were every step of the way. It was simply fascinating to see the area I was so familiar with from the air.

We flew south along the coast to Plymouth Harbor, where Peter pointed out the ribs of a ship that had run aground in the 1800s. We flew over the Cape Cod Canal, where barges were slowly being pushed along by tugboats. Peter banked the plane to the right, and we headed north over land back to Monponsett Pond, ending our flight with a gentle landing on smooth water.

That fantastic scenic tour planted another seed in me that day and started me thinking I had found a possible future for myself. I was restless working in an office every day and started searching for something new and different.

One day while working in my office, Bobby, one of the family members who owned the supermarket chain, stopped by to say hi. I was never quite sure what his motives were, but I enjoyed the distraction and interaction. After I greeted him, he said, "It's obvious you do an excellent job here, but you appear to need something more challenging."

Finally, I thought, I was being recognized as being worth more, and I agreed with him. I knew I needed something different, but honestly, I had no idea what that was. I thought about a better future all the time, looking at courses I could take in the evening, reading want ads in the local newspaper, watching other employees while they were doing their jobs. I never saw anything that interested me in the least.

In the office, when I finished whatever project I was working on, I looked for more work. It was impossible for me to pretend to work as I had seen the other girls do when I first came up to the main office.

Bobby continued, "There's a workbook called *What Color Is Your Parachute?* And I think it will be helpful to you."

"Thank you," I said politely, but inwardly thinking, What on earth are you talking about?

It never occurred to me that they wanted to know where I would be better suited in their company. I'm glad I didn't know. While I was happy to be working to support my family, I wasn't challenged or thrilled by the work I was doing.

I bought the workbook, thinking, This is going to answer so many of my questions.

On Saturday morning, I sat down at the kitchen table and got to work. I kept answering questions and wondered how the process was going to turn into anything of value. When I was finished answering the questions, the results were surprising to me. They told me I wanted to be a commercial seaplane charter pilot.

But I wasn't a pilot and had no idea how to become one.

But then I thought: The family I worked for owned a home on Lake Winnipesaukee in New Hampshire. Family members took turns going there for weeks at a time, and the fathers drove there on Friday evening, coming back to work early the following week. If I was a seaplane charter pilot, I could fly them to their vacation homes, saving them so much time and effort. But I felt they would never trust me to fly them since I was just one of their employees.

But that got the wheels turning in my mind—maybe other people who owned homes on the lake would be interested in a similar seaplane charter service.

I asked Peter, the seaplane pilot who had given my daughters and me our scenic ride, how I could become a seaplane pilot. "You have to become a land pilot first," he told me.

I didn't like his answer. I didn't want to be a land pilot. About a month later, I asked another acquaintance how to become a seaplane pilot. He echoed Peter: "You have to become a land pilot first." I didn't like his answer, either.

Not one to give up easily, I called the airport in Marshfield and asked them if they knew how to become a seaplane pilot. The manager said, "You have to become a land pilot first."

Not happy about the same answer, I felt it was time to give it up. I couldn't afford to become a land pilot. I needed to take care of my children.

I was adamant about giving them every opportunity to search for their passion in life and, like so many other mothers, thought my turn had passed. I was still married to Tony, but he wanted me to give him the money I made instead of spending it on the girls. That was not going to happen. I survived the worst year of my life after divorcing. I wanted the family to stay together, but I just couldn't hang on any longer. I was losing myself.

Several years went by. I survived several corporate buyouts and a divorce from my first husband and found myself working in the sales end of the industry for a food wholesaler. I finally had an opportunity to be creative, but still felt the need to be doing something else.

I had been going to Maine on weekends and realized how much I loved being outdoors. Whether it was hiking, backpacking, cross-country skiing, or riding my bike, I was much happier outside. I loved the smell of the fresh air, the process of dressing just right for the variety of conditions, and the feeling of my muscles when I had used them.

I had read somewhere that if you want to make a change in your career and don't know what you want to do, you need to give up the security you depend on. Items to let go were the weekly paycheck, the 401K, and health insurance. Not having the security of health insurance was the most frightening to give up. That sense of security was something I had—and needed—ever since I could remember.

In 1990, at the age of 45, it was finally time for me. Anna was 25 and living in California, and Lisa, 20, was finishing up at Union College. I remarried and was financially stable at that time, so I took the plunge and left my job. I sold my house and moved to Maine.

I moved into my new husband's old family camp and gave myself time to figure out what I was supposed to do with the rest of my life. I hiked, rode my bike, backpacked into the mountains, went snowshoeing and cross-country skiing for a year. That experience confirmed my need to be outside.

STARTING A NEW CHALLENGE

The following year, after all my time hiking, backpacking, and cross-country skiing in the vast woodlands of Maine, the local airport in Fryeburg was having its annual dinner meeting and open house. Lindsay, my second husband of two years, was the new selectman in Brownfield. Selectman is a New England term for an official in a rural town who makes decisions. With that responsibility also come perks, like being invited to the airport's dinner meeting. Fortuitously, I decided to tag along.

After dinner, the meeting continued for a short period of time, and then the president of the board announced scenic flights were available if anyone was interested. I certainly was. Tom, the pilot, was standing next to the podium. He was a short, confident-looking man with broad-rimmed glasses who was looking around the room for any passengers. Without hesitation, I walked up to the front of the room.

"I would love to go for a scenic flight," I said.

"Well, come with me; I would love to take you," he said.

We walked out onto the ramp and climbed aboard a tan plane with low wings. I settled into the right front seat. The pilot sat in the left. There were tan curtains on the back windows matching the fabric on the seats and all sorts of instruments I knew nothing about. I was quite impressed with those fancy curtains and thrilled to be on a new adventure to see the area I knew so well from the ground.

We took off heading toward magnificent snow-capped Mount Washington and gracefully turned 180 degrees in the opposite direction. As much as I loved the woods, I was surprised to see how much more beautiful it was from the air.

We flew toward a village I knew to be Hiram, right next to the Saco River with its church steeple majestically sticking up from the green trees. As I looked down from the plane, I could see the twists and turns as the river meandered along its way to the ocean. The water was lower than I anticipated, displaying the beaches along the shore where Lindsay and I had made several stops for a swim on a previous hot summer day.

It was early October during that flight, and the foliage carpeting the ground was an artistic display I could never have imagined. The combination of varying shades of yellow and red were highlighted by the surrounding crisp dark-green pine and spruce trees. This view left an impression on me I will never forget. I thought I was familiar with the woods from spending so much time outdoors, but I never expected to be unfamiliar with most of the area from the air.

When driving a car, it took 20 minutes to go 14 miles from Fryeburg to Hiram. By canoe, it took all day paddling as we followed every bend along the river. However, by plane we arrived in five minutes. My mind was buzzing.

"This is quite a sight Tom," I said. "The view is spectacular, and I feel as if I'm in a dream, drifting along and seeing all this beauty."

Tom smiled and said, "I feel very fortunate to share this experience with someone who appreciates it so much."

"Can a plane like this fly to Boston?" I asked.

Think of all the time I would save getting to Massachusetts to visit my family! My mind was spinning. Driving through Boston was a nightmare. It would take five hours on a rainy Friday afternoon to get to the South Shore. I would not only get there faster, I would have fun flying.

"Yes. You can fly wherever you want to go," he responded.

I asked, "Where did you learn how to fly?"

"Right here at the Fryeburg airport. By the expression on your face you look as though you might like to learn, too."

"I would like to ask some questions and consider it. I've been looking for something else to do. I love being outdoors and in the woods, but would enjoy a good challenge."

Tom turned the plane around and I could easily see the airport from where we were. He landed smoothly on the same runway we had left just minutes before.

"I would like to speak to someone. How do I go about that?" I asked with just a bit of trepidation. I knew I wouldn't do well if I was forced into a specific timeframe, as I hated to be under pressure to get something done—along with the fact that I certainly didn't want to fail.

"You can take lessons right here. You can go at your own pace and enjoy the learning experience," Tom said. "I'll introduce you to an instructor after we stop."

I had been looking for something more constructive to do with all my free time and thought this was a good choice.

In my quest to figure out what I wanted to do with the rest of my life, becoming a commercial seaplane charter pilot had become a forgotten memory. I had totally given up that goal. You would think I would have been reminded of those thoughts during this experience, but I was 46 and never gave any consideration to the possibility of becoming a pilot at that age.

After starting lessons, there was no stopping me. It was the first time in my life that there was no question as to what I wanted to do. I was 47 (my birthday was in December) when I got my private pilot's certificate in 1992, and I thought that was an enormous accomplishment.

I managed to get it in six months, but after that, I knew I needed to fly better. I wanted to feel as comfortable in the plane as I did when driving my car. I had not accomplished that with a private pilot certificate.

I decided to continue with my flight training and get an instrument rating. That would allow me to fly in all kinds of weather, relying on the cockpit instruments for navigation and safety. It was intense work, and I was scared to think I would have to fly in the clouds and down to 200 feet above the ground on my own. Those thoughts led me to make excuses that I really didn't want an instrument rating.

When I got stuck in Albany, New York, after visiting with Lisa at school, and without the ability I needed to get through 1,000 feet of clouds to get on top and fly home, I was motivated to get to work. At that time, I had a one-fifth ownership in a Piper Archer that was great to fly and equipped for instrument work and cross-country flights. It happened to be the very same plane I'd had the scenic flight in after the dinner meeting in Fryeburg—the one with the pretty curtains that matched the fabric on the seats.

BEGINNING OF A NEW LIFE

In flying, I had finally found something that gave me great satisfaction. It also encouraged me, proving that I was capable of accomplishing something greater than I ever had before.

My mother, of course, didn't approve. She never asked how my lessons were going, nor did she ever acknowledge the fact that I was a private pilot. That was an insult to me and made me more determined to be a good pilot.

If I worked hard enough, I could become a good, safe instrument-rated pilot. Learning to fly was not easy, but when you "get it," the feeling of euphoria is beyond description.

Learning to fly on instruments requires the same amount of time it takes to get a private pilot's license, about 40 hours. It is challenging, but the clouds were no longer going to hold me back from getting where I wanted to go.

During one of my first instrument flight lessons, my instructor reached into his pocket and pulled out breath mints.

"Would you like a mint, Mary?"

"No thanks," I said. I thought he had bad breath, but it never occurred to me that I did!

This led me to thinking that if my husband smelled like he was saturated with alcohol all the time, then perhaps I did too. I certainly didn't want anyone to think I was drinking while flying, so I decided to reduce the number of drinks I had at night and stop smoking. I didn't want to have bad breath.

I wanted people to want to be with me in a plane and not smell like a barroom. My addiction to cigarettes had to go. The ritual of five p.m. came around the next day after the "mint" offer, and my husband Lindsay asked, "Can I make you a drink?"

"No thanks. I've made it all day without smoking, and if I have a drink now, I'll smoke." At that time, I drank every day and always too much.

In the evening, I could never answer the phone when my daughter from California called because my words would be slurred, and I didn't want her to hear me like that.

That night, I worked on a project on my computer, which was in a room down in the cellar. After dinner, just to keep myself busy, I worked until I was exhausted. I dragged myself up the stairs and went into the living room to watch TV, and as soon as I sat down on the couch, I immediately got right up and went back to the computer. I could not sit still. I needed to stay preoccupied to keep my mind off having a cigarette and a drink. I went to bed exhausted that night and not sure I could endure another night of such intense anxiety.

I woke up the next morning with some comprehension of the effects of alcohol. Somewhere I had heard, "It's the first drink that creates the problem." I had tried for five years to control my drinking, but it was controlling me. As soon as I had that first drink, an obsession kicked in and I couldn't stop.

That next morning, I was on a campaign to stop Lindsay from drinking. Actually, I was insane that following morning, but I didn't know it. Why I thought I needed to control him, I don't know. My mind was racing, and I was walking around in circles, anxious, confused, and out of control.

I called an 800 number I found in the phone book (no cell phones at this time) for people who wanted information about stopping drinking, and a very nice woman said, "Oh, you need to speak with someone else who can help you with that." I hung up on her. I've never hung up on anyone in my life, so I was quite surprised at my response. I then called that same 800 number again, and this time a mature-sounding man answered the phone. I liked what he had to say. At least I didn't hang up on him.

"Usually in the first stages of sobriety, it is recommended you see an alcoholic counselor," he said. "There are many reasons we all drink, and without the drink, we need to do something about the underlying issues."

Three years earlier, a doctor at the Bridgton Hospital had spoken to me about my drinking. I needed to have surgery on my neck, and when filling out the forms, I put down honestly that I had six or seven drinks a day. What I didn't realize was that people normally lie on those forms and the authorities double what you say! Fortunately, I didn't know that at the time.

"Mary, have you ever thought about doing anything about your drinking?" the doctor asked.

"No," I said with confidence and a smile.

He continued in a kind, matter-of-fact manner, "Well, if you ever do, we have a very successful program here at the hospital that you might find helpful."

This little "seed," deeply planted, was slow to sprout. I liked the sound of hospital care, as I was brought up depending on medicine and hospitals. My uncle was a doctor and my mother a wannabe nurse.

After speaking with the volunteer on the phone, I called the hospital and set up an appointment. About a month later, this kind, tall stout man tried to convince me to go to a meeting where other people shared their strength and experience during their drinking days and after. I wanted no part of this: I did not want anyone to think I was an alcoholic. Little did I know that it had been evident for years whenever I was out in the public.

My first AA meeting was in Norway, Maine, just far enough away from home that I would not be seen by anyone I knew. I parked the car along the side of the road and walked toward the group standing around outside the church where the meeting was being held. The men and women were chatting with each other and appeared happy to see their friends while hugging away. I hope no one hugs me! I immediately thought.

I walked right past them with my shoulders back and head held high. I didn't smoke any longer and they did. I'm sure my air of superiority was to hide my insecurity. I pretended I was "better than" for months until I realized I was no different from anyone else.

When I walked in, I looked for a seat by myself, but most of the chairs were full. Fortunately, I did not see any familiar faces. I sat down beside a bearded man who simply smiled at me and left me alone. I was happy with that. Months later, I found out they were all there for the same reason I was: to stay sober and concentrate on their own issues.

I didn't know about a reward system that AA had, and when they announced that anyone with a month of sobriety could come up and get a white chip, I walked up to the front of the room and came back to my seat. The bearded man next to me leaned over and shook my hand.

Three months later, I found out that the man I'd chosen to sit beside at my first meeting was the same man I'd spoken with on the first day I called the alcohol help line. This was a powerful message for me. On the night of my first meeting, and out of the 50 to 75 people in that room, I chose to sit beside the one and only person I had spoken to in this program. I knew then I was doing the right thing and that I was guided by a much higher power. I want to stay on this path, I thought. One of the many things I learned in AA is that there is no such thing as a coincidence.

I've stayed sober during divorce and threats to my life with the strength of the people I met in this community. It was important to choose a sponsor, and I did. However, she was not equipped to deal with the issues I had with my mother.

"Mary, there is a woman counselor in East Baldwin who specializes in working with alcoholics and people dealing with alcoholics in the family. I think you would get a great deal out of meeting with her," she said. I did and started my journey to becoming the woman I was meant to be.

I was familiar with the addiction to smoking. I had stopped for five years on two previous occasions. I knew my addiction to alcohol was exactly like that of smoking. At first, the smell of smoke was obnoxious. Then I would borrow a cigarette on the weekend to have with a drink while dining out. Then, I would buy a pack and smoke outside, so as not to bother anyone in the house. Finally, in a very short period, I was smoking a pack a day, and it did not matter where I was when I did. I knew from that experience that if I had the glass of wine that I occasionally thought was a good idea, I would be back drinking again. I have now been 26 years without a cigarette or any alcohol.

Over these past 26 years I have occasionally thought it would be nice to have a drink while having dinner with friends. I am certain I would do just that at first, then two, until I was drinking to excess again every day. It would bring me back to being obnoxious, saying things I would regret the next morning and feeling miserable. It would also stop me from joining others hiking or skiing, but more importantly, I would not feel up to flying.

With the possibility of a new self-image—one where I had self-respect—smoking and drinking simply did not go along with what I expected of myself. Self-respect was sought after but continued to be an elusive goal. The thought of giving up my daily drinks had not been a consideration because I was sure I could eventually control that aspect of my life. I had no intention of giving it up, but fortunately for me, giving up smoking meant I had to give up the drink. The two went hand in hand.

Alcohol was a tool to help me escape from troubles and an opportunity to express myself in a way that just did not happen without that loose tongue. My biggest complaint was my mother, and it did not matter to me if someone wanted to listen or not. If someone tried to stop me, I raised my voice and became more belligerent. In any conversation, I was sure I was right. When it came to driving, I knew I would be the better driver, especially after drinking.

When I stopped drinking, I needed to do something about the festering hatred of my mother. I knew the only way to deal with this issue was to take my friend's suggestion and see a therapist. I did not want to drink again.

As it turned out, drinking was a gift that got me back to therapy. I now look at many bad experiences as gifts because they force me to make changes in my life.

I am and will always be grateful that aviation has wound its way into my life and given me the incentive to be a better person. Flying makes me feel whole. It's a constant job trying to be different than I was for years, but I keep trying.

WHAT'S NEXT?

"What are you going to do next Mary?"

When I was finished with my instrument rating, I ran into Charlie Peck, a pilot who flew to Fryeburg from Portland every day. He brought his lunch with him and sat at the picnic table under the pine trees in the nice cool shade. He enjoyed the comings and goings of all the planes and chatting with the local pilots. He was always in a conversation with someone and loved to have me join him. I soon realized that once I had passed my test, known as a check-ride, and became a private pilot, other pilots were interested in talking to me. Prior to that, they just smiled and passed right by.

Charlie was of medium height and sported an Irish tweed cap and a well-worn green wool sweater with burn holes in it from smoking his cigar. He was scruffy, but he showed interest in my accomplishments as a pilot and I loved sharing stories with him.

When I told him I had my instrument rating, he said, "What are you going to do next, Mary?"

"I'm all done, Charlie," I told him. "I wanted to fly better, and I feel I've accomplished that. I've also just spent a lot of money."

"Well, how about a Commercial Rating?"

"What on earth am I going to do with a Commercial Rating at fifty years old?" I asked.

"Well, you would be a better pilot."

This ruffled my feathers more than you can imagine. My face got red, something I could never stop from happening when I was upset, and my facial expression changed from a smile to one of dismay. I never could hide my emotions. I thought he meant I wasn't a good pilot, that I had to prove myself. Then I thought, if Charlie thinks I'm a bad pilot, other pilots must be thinking the same thing.

I scurried right out and spent the next two weeks getting ten hours of "complex" training, earning my Commercial Rating. *Complex* means flying a plane with retractable gear and a variable-pitch propeller. This adjustable propeller allows a plane to perform at its best when climbing out after takeoff and then faster when in cruise.

The next time I saw Charlie at the airport, he asked, "What are you going to do next?" Charlie was persistent.

"Nothing!" I said.

"What about a seaplane rating?"

Little did I know he was sending me on a path I never would have imagined. He was the first of my mentors.

I almost fell over. "I wanted to do that years ago and had forgotten all about it. Where can I go to get that?" I asked.

"Twitchell's Airport in Turner is where they specialize in seaplane ratings," he said.

During the next two weeks, I flew over to Twitchell's Airport and took seaplane lessons. I arrived at the airport in my one-fifth ownership of the Archer (the one with the pretty curtains and matching upholstery).

When I arrived, Dale Twitchell said the keys were in his truck and gave me directions to the seaplane base. I had never been in a truck, but didn't hesitate to hop in and drive it—nothing like a new adventure. I drove down through the field where the corn was showing its yellow fans indicating it was time to be picked. Just the tops were swaying gently in the breeze. When I arrived at the seaplane base, the mist was rising from the water with the sun shining above, creating rainbows everywhere. I was in heaven.

First, my young female instructor showed me the importance of keeping the front of the floats up when taxiing out of the cove so the propeller would not hit the water. I didn't think it was a big deal, but when not done correctly, the water could potentially take chips right out of that metal blade.

The instructor then showed me a normal takeoff and landing. That was pretty basic: I had to get the plane going fast enough on the water to ease the plane off the water by pulling gently back on the yoke. Landing was a little more of an issue because the front of the floats would dig into the water, making it very uncomfortable (and a little scary). So, when landing, the yoke had to be gently pulled back to keep that from happening. I went through many of those with her and was turned loose to practice after an hour and a half.

Then I learned how to land in rough water and confined spaces, and to perform a variety of maneuvers *on* the water. It turned out that the handling on the water was interesting because there are no brakes when the plane is on water. I had to think through what the wind was going to do so I could get to the dock. I had to shut down and coast to the dock, jump out, and secure the plane. It was a wonderful adventure.

Once I was set free, I loved the independence of not asking for any help when preparing the plane for flight. This process is called a preflight, and I always needed help with my plane on wheels at the airport. It was in a hangar and too heavy for me to pull out onto the ramp. I disliked asking someone from the maintenance shop to help me pull it out, and the manager didn't like it either.

With the seaplane, I could untie it, turn it around, and secure it again to inspect the other side. Then I could untie it again, easily push the plane away from the dock, and hop in to start it. You can't start a seaplane while it's tied to the dock and expect to go anywhere. The ropes would become so tight it would be impossible to untie.

On my first solo excursion, a bald eagle gracefully flew from the side of the small cove where the planes were kept toward the river, showing me the way. I felt as if I was guided by him. I don't ever remember feeling like that, but I knew I belonged right there, flying by myself in a seaplane. There is no other way to explain it. I was more comfortable with myself than ever before. I'd grown up in the little coastal town of Cohasset and spent most of my leisure time on or near the water. The combination of being on the water and flying filled my soul.

After five more hours of flight training at the seaplane base, learning how to land on the water in varying conditions, it was time to go for a check-ride. That's when an FAA Designated Examiner comes to the base to test you in the plane to make sure you are safe to fly on floats.

When the examiner arrived, he asked if I was a commercial pilot.

"I am," I said.

"Well then, I'll give you a commercial seaplane check-ride."

As a commercial pilot, I was going to be allowed to take passengers, so I had to be more precise than a private pilot.

"I haven't practiced any commercial maneuvers," I said nervously.

"Don't worry, I'm sure you'll be fine."

I thought that if I had to do lazy eights, chandelles, and eights on pylons, I'd be in trouble. Those maneuvers are a combination of flying with varying airspeeds, altitudes, and headings. They demonstrate that the pilot can fly in a variety of configurations to the limit of the airplane, while staying in control and dividing her attention. I later found out these maneuvers are not required for a seaplane add-on rating. If I were going for the original commercial rating as I did on wheels, those maneuvers would be mandatory.

The examiner was right—I earned my commercial seaplane rating that day, fulfilling a dream I had had so many years ago.

As I was flying home, I couldn't believe I was now a commercial seaplane pilot. I was thrilled beyond belief.

MUST GET TO WORK

The following week, Neil, my airplane mechanic, informed me that a seaplane was for sale and at a good price. The owner called me to discuss it, but I didn't know the first thing about buying a seaplane. Everyone who talked to me about it had something to gain, and I didn't know who to trust.

Neil could see my hesitation but knew that plane was just right for me. He had done the maintenance on it over many years and wanted to help the seller.

"There's a guy over in Naples who is undoubtedly the best seaplane pilot in the state of Maine and knows the most about general aviation aircraft because he buys and sells them all the time," Neil advised. "He may be a little grouchy, but I think he will help you."

He gave me his number. I'm not sure I even knew this guy's name at that time, so I called and told him all I knew about the Cessna 172 with a 180-hp engine on PK 2300 floats that was for sale. He said it certainly sounded good to him and he would take a look at it for me.

"If it's the plane I think it is, you should take advantage of the situation, especially since Neil has been the mechanic for years," he added.

After that conversation, I trusted Neil's opinion about the airplane, and I bought it.

The insurance company required that I get ten hours of flight training in that plane prior to flying solo, a common requirement for companies that insure airplanes. I thought I would go to Rangeley to see another part of Maine and fly in and out of the lakes there.

I got a different experience, all right. The wind whipped the lakes into a frenzy, and I had my hands full. One day, my instructor had me pull up to a beach along the southwest shore of one of the larger lakes. The wind was behind us, along with whitecaps rolling off the huge (to me) waves on the rough water. We both climbed out of the plane onto the floats and hopped onto the beach. He was going to teach me how to "beach" and secure a seaplane.

"Now, be careful when we start to turn it. It's going to come around fast," he said.

I didn't have a clue how fast that was going to happen. We pushed the plane back off the sand so it would float and barely started it turning on the water when it swung around, nearly knocking me over as I ducked to avoid the tail coming over my head.

That left an impression of respect for the wind with a seaplane. I was scared for the first time and have never forgotten how important it was for me to understand different conditions and not just calm winds.

Soon after I purchased the plane, Howard Dearborn, an entrepreneur from Fryeburg, said, "I understand you bought a seaplane."

"I did!"

"Where are you going to keep it?"

"I don't have a clue!"

Sounds dumb, doesn't it? Anyway, he told me I could keep it at his place on Lovewell Pond if I wanted to.

When I finished with the ten hours of training in Rangeley, I flew to Lovewell Pond with much more confidence and a new respect for the trouble I could get myself into. When I arrived, I found Howard clearing a place for me with his tractor and making sure I had everything I needed to secure the plane. I only lived three miles away, and this was a perfect solution.

I was on a dreamlike journey...one I never expected to enjoy so much. There was no hesitation in my mind about learning all I could about flying seaplanes.

I was going to fly. There was no question about that. I decided I had better find a way to put my commercial seaplane rating to good use, because I couldn't continue to spend money that fast. I needed to start making it instead.

THE PROMISE

On my first seaplane charter flight in 1997, I realized I had reached my previously forgotten goal of becoming a Commercial Seaplane Charter Pilot, without consciously working toward it. I felt euphoric when I became aware of this. Right then, I promised myself that I would continue to follow my path in aviation and hoped more opportunities would present themselves to me when the time was right.

As if on cue, John Wood, my FAA inspector, came to the Naples Seaplane Base (76B) for my Part 135 Seaplane Charter inspection. Everything went well during our flight. Afterwards, he asked, "Mary, would you be willing to be a CFI?" Aviation is filled with abbreviations, and this one stands for Certified Flight Instructor.

"No, I don't think so, John. I don't think I want to be a flight instructor. I'm quite happy here doing scenic flights and charters."

"I hope you'll consider getting this rating. We're happy with the condition you keep your equipment in, and we need a place to fly and stay current with seaplane operations."

Just like the rest of general aviation pilots, FAA employees must stay current in order to do any inspections with the district charter pilots.

On the way home that night, I realized I had to live up to my promise to myself to continue to follow my path in aviation. I decided to get that instructor rating.

During business hours the following day, I called American Flyers in New York for information. They had a good reputation for preparing pilots to become flight instructors. I had worked on all my other ratings with a local instructor and studied on my own. For this rating, I knew I needed more help to become an instructor.

Both of my parents were teachers. Dad taught a Naval Intelligence class every Thursday night in the Fargo Building in Boston. Mother had her master's degree in education and specialized in dyslexia in the Hingham, Massachusetts, school system.

Teaching was not something I'd ever considered as a path for me. In high school, I looked up to the front of the room and saw a person who was enthusiastic about their job. I wondered how on earth someone would want to teach kids who didn't want to be sitting in that room. I know *I* didn't want to be there. Again, I had no idea what I wanted at that time, but it certainly wasn't teaching. It never occurred to me that teaching someone who was motivated to learn could be fun.

After getting accepted at American Flyers, I closed the seaplane base in October and drove to Long Island to start my "30 days" of training. I had images of coming home after 30 days as a flight instructor, but those "30 days" turned out to be only the ground school. I never got near an airplane until December.

I joined a group of four students and started with the classes for my Certified Flight Instrument Instructor rating (CFII). They did the CFII first for a variety of reasons. I assumed they wanted to keep their students, but their explanation was that the CFI (Certified Flight Instructor) would then become an "add-on" and less complicated to complete. Not sure what I would ever do with an Instrument Instructor rating as a seaplane pilot, but again my promise to myself was looming. This was the way American Flyers taught, and I was there to learn.

One day, our assignment was to pick a lesson to teach the class. We needed to choose something we were familiar with in order to show our teaching style. It was to have nothing to do with aviation.

I was staying in a convent where my Aunt Kate was a nun. It was a very peaceful place that was perfect for spending time alone to study and go to mass every morning. I had asked if I could stay there during my flight training and was welcomed with open arms.

I was racking my brain to think of what to bring to use as a teaching tool for class. As I walked through the dimly lit dining room that evening looking for anything familiar, I walked into the laundry room and saw an iron and an ironing board. A light bulb went off in my head. That was something I was quite familiar with.

The following morning, I asked permission from one of the nuns to borrow both, grabbing a sprinkler and spray starch for good measure. I put them in my car and drove to class. One of the instructors always came to class with a shirt and tie, but the shirt was always a wrinkled mess. I was going to teach him how to iron. This was one of the few times that I thanked my mother for hovering over my shoulder. He needed to learn how to iron.

Joel, one of my fellow students, was first and proceeded to show us how to build a set of stairs. He definitely knew what he was talking about, but I didn't get what he was trying to say and didn't learn how to build stairs. The other three men in the class probably did, but I wasn't going to be a carpenter.

Next, Ivan tried in vain to tell us how to fly an Antonov An-22 Russian plane that he had evidently flown. First of all, it wasn't supposed to be anything about aviation, and secondly, he failed. He was disorganized, spoke too softly, and showed no interest in teaching. However, he did tell us all about himself and how well he flew the plane. Great. How are they going to respond to learning how to iron if I don't care about either of these two subjects?

When my turn came, I gathered my set of tools and went to the front of the room. While setting up the ironing board, my presentation started with, "Now all of you are going to be flight instructors, and the condition in which you present yourself to your students is important. A wrinkled shirt shows you are sloppy, and you will therefore be less respected." (Words from my mother for sure.)

First, I sprinkled one of my wrinkled cotton button-down shirts and rolled it up while I explained the importance of getting better results with the garment evenly dampened. As the moisture was spreading through my shirt, my iron was heating up for the next step. When the iron was hot enough, I put the shirt on the ironing board and started to press the back of the collar.

Everyone in the room, including the instructor with the messy shirt, came right up to see what I was doing. No one in the class had ever successfully ironed a shirt. Feeling elated, I then moved on to the first sleeve while talking and talking. Not sure what I said, but everyone stayed glued to what I was doing. Surprisingly, I had an enthusiastic audience.

Peter, one of my friends in class, asked how to manage the shoulder. He said he never could fit it on the board. I asked him to show me what he normally did, and he used the end of the ironing board with the straight edge, the end where the iron rests when I iron.

I said, "See if you have better luck on this end." He moved my shirt to the other end, where the shoulder fit perfectly on the board. A smile of satisfaction crossed his face. He was thrilled.

As I concluded my demonstration, my classmates continued to ask questions. Unfortunately, the instructor never did get the message. He continued to come to class a wrinkled disaster.

I passed that lesson with flying colors. Deeply satisfied, I went back to the convent knowing I only needed to know what I was talking about, have motivated students, and teach them what I know and love to do.

Simple! I couldn't wait to finish my training, go back to Maine, and be a seaplane flight instructor.

FLIGHT INSTRUCTION

As a flight instructor, I had the pleasure of flying with many pilots, but the memories of some stand out more than others. Eric Faraday went on to become an airline captain, Chad Guilford instructs F-18 pilots on and off carriers, Stefen Lind is a seaplane flight instructor teaching students to fly customers onto the East River in New York City after flying in Ketchikan, Alaska, and Kenmore Air Harbor, Seattle. Matt McFadden worked for me for eight years and eventually took over the seaplane base on Long Lake where I started my career with seaplanes. Each one of those students loved to be challenged and to experience everything they could in aviation. The longest relationship was with Matt, who came to work for me in 2005.

In the spring of that year, I was lying on my hospital bed in my office, just home from my first hip replacement. I was delighted when my business phone rang (no cell phone in those days). I needed every diversion I could to keep me sane. I was not good at being inactive.

"Good morning, Naples Seaplane Service."

"Good morning. I would like to discuss getting a seaplane rating." This was a common call those days—and in March I was more than happy to start scheduling lessons for June.

I gave my usual information about the approximate time it would take (six to eight hours) to get the rating, and he asked about scheduling an appointment to get started.

"Could you tell me a little about yourself and your experience flying?" I asked.

Matt went on to tell me about the number of hours he had flown, and that he was a mechanic and a flight instructor. A perfect fit for my operation.

"Well, if you're a flight instructor, why don't you come to work for me?"

After a long pause, Matt said, "I would like to think about that."

"That sounds good to me. If you decide to come, we open the season with a Seaplane Expo in the beginning of June. I'll need help preparing the grounds and setting up chairs in the hangar. If the weather is good, we can expect over a hundred people to attend. This year, we have the pilot that flew the C-130 to Antarctica to pick up a patient. The public is also invited to attend. We now have the facility for amphibious pilots to land on the water, taxi up the seaplane ramp, and park on the field. Many look forward to starting the season with a social and educational event. The FAA will be here to present a seaplane safety seminar."

Matt called several times after that conversation, asking a multitude of questions. I was happy to see he was not impulsive. His personality was what I was looking for in an instructor and a mechanic. However, he needed a place to stay.

I asked Arlene Stetson, who owned a B&B, The Augustus Bove House at the end of the driveway, if she had an extra room.

"Of course I do. He can have the top floor."

Matt was one of 12 children and the only one to not live close to home in Ohio. I wasn't sure he would stay very long, but I think he loved the seaplane base and his new way of life.

He eventually met his wonderful wife, Allison, and their wedding was at the seaplane base. One of Matt's brothers, playing his trumpet, presented the most reverent version of the Our Father that I've ever heard, while Matt and Allison stood under a flower-decorated arch next to the water. The hangar was used for the reception, decorated with a seaplane in the corner! Matt's whole family came, along with their spouses, and we all enjoyed a wonderful time dancing to a small band that played square dance music—a joyous event.

When he first arrived, I gave Matt the instruction he needed to get a seaplane rating, and he became proficient enough to be an instructor. When pilots came to the base for seaplane training, I was the one who had the reputation, and they wanted me to be their instructor. I wouldn't keep a flight instructor working for me very long if I took all the students, so I encouraged them to fly with Matt.

"This is what I would like you to do," I said to my customers. "If you will fly with Matt and you're not satisfied with his training, I will give you your money back and fly with you myself."

I never had anyone come back asking me to fly with them.

When I became an FAA Designated Examiner, Matt did all the flight training. He continues to run a very successful seaplane scenic flight business on Long Lake in Naples during the summer and works as a mechanic in Oxford during the winter, along with a variety of other jobs.

He is a very good pilot, knows the area like the back of his hand, and stays profitable by doing his own maintenance. Money can be made during the summer, but it normally flies out the window with maintenance during the winter. Matt can avoid most of those expenses by doing his own work. He is like a son to me. His children call me "Gramma Mary," which I adore.

Chad Guilford is another cherished student. When he was 15, I started flying with him when I was working as a flight instructor at the Auburn/Lewiston Airport. As we were flying, it was obvious to me how well he flew. I looked through his logbook. I was surprised that he hadn't flown for several months. I didn't know he was only 15 at the time.

"Chad, you could get through your training easily if you flew more often."

"Believe me, I wish I could fly more, but I'm busy in the summer."

I thought perhaps he went on vacation with his family or maybe to summer camp.

"What keeps you so busy?"

"I fish for lobsters."

"Oh," I said, "do you fish with your dad or grandfather?"

"No, I have my own boat."

I grew up in a lobstering town south of Boston, but never knew any kid this young to have his own lobster boat. When we finished flying and went into the office, I was very impressed when he took a checkbook out of his pocket and wrote a check for his flying lessons. I wanted to have this young man fly with me more often.

"I would like to help you fly on a regular basis. It's winter now, so we should be able to get a lot in before you fish and I go back to the seaplane base."

"Thank you," he said. "I would love that, but it's a long trip to get here and I don't drive yet."

I thought about what I could do and asked the head flight instructor if I could fly one of the school planes to Rockland to meet Chad so he could fly more often. The ferry came from Vinalhaven Island to Rockland on a regular basis, so he could get there by himself. The answer was no.

"Well, okay, but I really want to help this young man out so he can solo on his birthday, so I'll go there in one of my planes."

That didn't seem to upset anyone, and Chad was thrilled. He knew the FAA requirements were for him to be 16 before he could solo, and he wanted to solo on his birthday.

After our first lesson, Chad said, "Mary, I don't feel right having you come all this way to teach me. Can we meet halfway?"

"Sure, we can. How about meeting in Wiscasset?"

That seemed to satisfy him and make my expenses a little less, too. I didn't charge him to fly the plane to and from the airport where he was training.

When it came time to fly his required solo cross-country flights, I went for long walks or borrowed a car and went to lunch while waiting for him to return. I enjoyed every minute of helping this young man reach his goals.

He became a private pilot in my Super Cruiser just after his 17th birthday. I flew it home the day he finished his check-ride, landed in the field, and Matt immediately converted it into a seaplane for me. It was lifted off the hangar floor using the newly installed chain fall, the wheels and gear removed, and floats and struts installed. The process took about four hours. I had a student coming for a seaplane rating later in the week and needed it in that configuration.

Chad came the following week and worked on his seaplane rating and accomplished it in two and a half hours. It normally takes six to eight hours of training, but he was used to the plane, had grown up on the water with a lobstering family, and was very easy to train.

There were some seaplane students who came back each year to become more proficient, but Chad came as many weekends as he could to fly and build time when he was in high school. In aviation, experience is judged by the amount of time you have flying. It also includes what type of planes you've flown.

The first time we flew together on wheels out of our field, I took the controls from the instructor's seat in the back of the tandem Piper Super Cruiser. We landed several times with Chad at the controls for practice at a variety of local airports. We then headed back to Naples.

As we approached the base, I said, "Okay, I'll do the first landing onto the field."

He immediately responded, "I would like to do the landing in there." He was not intimidated in any way.

I explained where he needed to land and he continued to fly. I was also very clear about doing a go-around without hesitation if he was too high to land in front of the hangar. His landing was perfect. I was just as pleased as he was.

He came back in the winter and wanted to experience ski flying. His parents came to watch this time. I was happy to have them see where their son liked to come on weekends. I would, too, if I had a teenager who left for four or five weekends a year. He would normally arrive in time to join us for dinner and then sleep on the pull-out couch in the living room, anxious to fly the next day. It was a half-hour boat trip for him from the island of Vinalhaven to the mainland, and another two or more hours' drive to Naples.

The temperature was about 45 degrees that day, the sun shining brightly in a lovely clear blue sky. Although those conditions were perfect for flying, the snow was a little sticky.

"Chad, we may have a longer takeoff than normal today due to the conditions, so if you are not off the ground by the first hangar you need to abort your takeoff."

He always did what I told him, so I was quite confident in his ability to follow directions.

We taxied up as far as we could to the end of the field, turned around, and headed down the runway. He pushed the throttle forward, giving full power, but we just sort of chugged along, not building up our normal takeoff speed. When the tail lifts on a tailwheel plane on the takeoff roll, speed will pick up—the tail ski is not dragging in the snow and the wings are straighter, allowing the air to flow faster. The plane normally lifts off right after that tail lifting. I had my hand on my throttle control in the back ready to abort the takeoff.

Just before we reached the hangar, the tail lifted. I thought, Great, we're just going to make it. At the same time, Chad brought the stick back as he always did to lift off, but in those conditions, that brought the tail down, digging the tail ski into the sticky snow and we did not have enough speed to take off. We were going too fast to stop and not go into the four-foot bushes at the end of the runway. Chad guided the plane slightly to the right, down the ramp, building more speed, and lifted off. We were perfectly safe, but I had certainly never taken off like that before.

"I'm so sorry, I'm so sorry, Mary. I'm so sorry, I'm so sorry, I'm so sorry."

"Just keep flying, Chad, we're all right. Just keep flying."

The normal engine in that plane was 160 horsepower. It had just recently been taken out for an overhaul and a spare 150 horsepower engine installed. I knew a different engine was in the plane, but I assumed it was the same horsepower as the engine that was removed. When changing the engine, they needed to change the propeller that was approved for that combination. I didn't know that had been changed, too. The normal one that was on there had a better pitch for taking off quicker on skis. The combination of the less powerful engine, the different propeller, sticky conditions, and my hesitation to pull the power sooner created this close encounter with disaster.

I can't imagine what his poor parents were thinking as they saw this very poor demonstration of taking off on skis. Experienced pilots get a good chuckle out of this story, but I don't imagine Chad's parents were terribly impressed. I never dared to ask what they thought.

Chad is now in the Navy and a flight instructor teaching other pilots to fly F-18s on and off carriers.

"I couldn't have imagined a better way to earn my private pilot's license and get my start in aviation," Chad says today. "Beyond the flight training, what's even more important to me is the friendship and mentorship that was developed. I would go on to get my seaplane rating with Mary, and eventually work at the seaplane base, spending the majority of my summer there.

"To this day, my time spent working at the seaplane base with Mary and everyone there remains my fondest aviation experience. Despite moving on to a career in the Navy, it's all those experiences that I feel most shaped me and gave me the ability to be successful. I have Mary to thank for that, and I know I'm not the only one."

Throughout my flight instructing career, I have been blessed with students who were hardworking and dedicated.

FLYING TO ALASKA

When I first started flying, I wanted to go somewhere. It didn't matter where. I just wanted to get out of the practice area around the Fryeburg Airport. As beautiful as the area is with the snow-capped White Mountains to the west, the Atlantic Ocean clearly reflecting the rising sun to the east, and lush green farmland below, I had to move on.

It wasn't about the destination; it was the challenge of flight planning I enjoyed. Taking into consideration weather, terrain, landmarks, and timing was fun for me. I longed for multiple legs and perhaps many days of flying. Maybe I could fly to the Bahamas or Alaska?

1-800-992-7433 was imprinted on my brain. That is the phone number for the Flight Service Station (FSS) to obtain all the information I needed to prepare for a flight to another airport. It's like planning a road trip except that, flying a plane, you can go in a straight line from one airport to another.

Things to consider are distance, amount of time, heading, and fuel burn. Airplanes are restricted by the amount of fuel they carry, the amount of time it takes to burn that fuel, and not necessarily the distance to be flown. It all depends on whether there is a headwind slowing you down or a good tailwind speeding you up.

I became quite used to writing down in my version of shorthand the details I needed to plan my flight. The Flight Service person on the other end of the phone shot out that information like he was trying to put out a fire, and I wanted to be professional and get it the first time around. He or she would slow down if they were asked, but I wanted to fit right in as if I did that every day.

In the U.S., pilots aren't required to file a flight plan, but in Canada, pilots are required to file a VFR (visual flight rules) flight plan for every cross-country flight where the pilot is flying more than 25 nautical miles from the departure airport or when operating between Canada and the United States. (Copies of FAA and Nav Canada flight plans are at the end

51

of this chapter.) At certain airports, special requirements and/or procedures are in effect. These requirements and procedures are listed in the
Canada Flight Supplement and the Water Aerodrome Supplement.

In the U.S., what used to be called an Airport Flight Directory is now
called a Chart Supplement. These supplements are divided by sections of
the country: Northeast, Southeast, etc. However, today most pilots use
electronic flight programs such as ForeFlight or Garmin Pilot. Some use
printed products to back up their electronic devices. Those documents are
necessary because each airport has different runway configurations, various
frequencies to be used for getting the weather, and designated frequencies
for communicating with other pilots and airport personnel. Some airports
have air traffic control towers, while at others, pilots broadcast their intentions over the specified frequency.

For a towered airport, the order of getting information and broadcasting is: Get the weather, contact approach on a different frequency, and that
person will turn you over to the tower on a different frequency about ten
miles from the airport. Having that information in front of you in written
form is very helpful.

Brief comments are mandatory at a busy airport. When contacting
approach, pilots are to say who they are (type of airplane and registration
number), where they are (so many miles northeast, southeast, etc.), their
altitude, and their intentions ("inbound and landing" if doing so). In my
plane, if I were flying to Portland, Maine, I would say, "Portland Approach,
N4433M, fifteen northwest, inbound and landing."

There is duplication in advanced avionics (a selection of navigation
radios) in many planes today for any instrument flights. A laptop can run
out of battery power, but the avionics permanently installed in the plane are
more stable and updated every 28 days using programs purchased annually.
An SD card is used to download the updated details from a computer
and then transfer them to the airplane on a regular basis. I was fortunate to have good equipment in my plane. I wanted the flexibility to fly in
instrument conditions.

Prior to planning an extended trip to Alaska, I only needed VFR charts,
but the scale was too small to get a better picture of the whole route. Starting
with the WAC chart (World Aeronautical Chart), I used an erasable pink

highlighter to draw a route that was later transferred to the VFR chart. I started with a yellow highlighter when I first started flying, but found it could not be easily seen in the plane.

When planning a trip to Alaska in 2005, I needed four printed WAC Charts using a scale of 1:1,000,000, or 13.7 miles to an inch; ten VFR Charts (divided by various states) with a scale of 1:500,000, or 6.86 miles to an inch; four Airport/Facility Flight Directories (divided by sections of the country); instrument charts for all the airport areas we would be flying through; and instrument approach plates (showing the route to be flown into a given runway when you cannot see out the window) for the U.S.

Fortunately, there was one chart for Alaska's Alcan Highway due to the frequency of that trip being made by private pilots. So, instead of potentially using ten more VFR charts, one chart covered the 1,600-mile highway, making it easier to plan and follow our route. No need to continually switch from chart to chart when only part of the highway was in a corner of that chart. A very large case of charts was behind the front seat where it could be reached easily. I had all the charts numbered from Maine to Alaska, so it would be easy to select the next appropriate chart. The cost for all these charts, if I remember correctly, was in the vicinity of $250.

Today, with modern technology readily available, computer programs at a fee of $200 for the year make that process much simpler. That fee includes all the IFR updates that come in every 28 days. Using my home computer, I download the update onto an SD card and then insert that card in the instrument drive in the airplane. Prior to a flight now, using my iPad, I type in the departure and destination airport, then enter the time of intended departure and the altitude I plan on flying. The information I need for the flight is automatically calculated: The magnetic heading, distance, and even fuel consumption is there in seconds.

What used to take me hours of flight planning in 1992 now takes me no more than half an hour to plan one of my trips from Maine to Alaska. Each of the four times I've flown that trip, it has been easier with the advanced avionics available at my fingertips.

Another valuable bit of information that was available to me in my plane at the time was the current weather. Having radar visible on the navigation screen was invaluable. When flying in the western mountains of Canada, the only weather available to pilots is what exists at the time. The mountains prohibit any forecasting. Radio frequencies travel without obstructions and the mountains provide the limiting factors.

I'm comfortable giving seminars on flying west across the country, northwest through Canada, and then back into the United States when crossing the Alaskan border. However, the first time, just the thought of that trip stopped me in my tracks. Was I capable of flying a trip like that in a single-engine plane? The answer came one evening at a local Katahdin Wings meeting when a speaker presented a slide show describing his trip to Alaska in a Cessna 172. That was the same make and model of plane I flew at that time, so I knew I could enjoy that adventure, too.

Our First Trip to Alaska

In 2005, seven years after that inspiring slide show, the opportunity to fly to Alaska became a possibility. My third husband, Jim, and I decided to fly to Anchorage to attend the Alaska Airmen's Association Expo in May. We did business with most of the vendors and wanted to meet them and see their places of operation. Visiting those plants would require a lot of flying because they were so spread out, and some of them were great distances from Anchorage.

When planning the trip, many questions came up: Where should we stop for fuel? Should we make reservations at hotels ahead of our arrival? (We never did, but some people are more comfortable making those reservations.) What were the best cities to clear customs? What route would be the most efficient? Were there any special requirements for us to follow in Canada and Alaska? I was so excited about the prospect of doing all that planning. What thrilled me the most was having an airplane in Alaska to fly and see more of the majesty of the mountains, glaciers, and remote gravel airports, along with a close and personal view of Mount McKinley.

Emergency equipment was necessary. Using my desktop computer, I found websites listing all the mandatory items that had to be in the plane. To fly through Canada, we needed a rifle. Great—the thought of possibly being injured in the wilderness and needing a gun to keep bears from eating me was a little unsettling. In Alaska, we also needed a firearm, which could be a handgun, but that was not allowed in Canada. Was I getting myself into more than I had bargained for?

Camping, with the thought of guarding myself from predators, would create a sleepless night for sure. A hungry bear coming out of hibernation in May was not an animal I wanted to visit me during the night. However, if I was going to go down in some remote part of the world where no one could find me, I was going to have what I needed to survive. That meant having the required four days of food, water, and first aid, along with a firearm. The lists for the U.S. and Canada are available on several aviation websites.

In an effort to find the most direct route, I decided to fly from Maine to Montreal to clear customs on the way out, then west to clear customs in Sault Ste. Marie, Michigan, when arriving back in the States again.

The process for clearing customs was to call them an hour before our departure and let them know what time we planned to arrive at our destination. During that conversation, the number of people aboard the airplane was given, along with our passport numbers. It was not acceptable to arrive any more than 15 minutes prior to your stated arrival time. At some airports, the customs officers had to travel a distance to get there, and they definitely did not want you there before they got there. We were told to sit in the plane and wait if they had not yet arrived.

From Sault Ste. Marie, the plan was to fly as straight as possible to Cut Bank, Montana, with several stops along the way for fuel, food, and sometimes overnight stays. From there, we crossed the border into Canada and cleared customs at Lethbridge, the first airport of entry when crossing. At that airport, we were to pull up to a red or yellow outlined box on the pavement and used the red phone to call customs. They cleared us through Canada and gave us an authorization number to be used until we reached Alaska. We cleared customs again in Northway, Alaska.

I had heard how pilots followed the Alcan Highway that wound around the mountainous terrain for safety. The highway was started in March of 1942 by the U.S. Army Corps of Engineers at Dawson Creek, British Columbia, to connect at Delta Junction, Alaska. It is 1,600 miles long and took 11,000 soldiers and eight months to build. The airports along that road are normally 250 miles apart. At the Watson Lake Airport in Yukon,

Canada, there are several pictures showing the construction of the road. Many local residents helped design and build the highway, because they knew the area and how best to travel through it.

I didn't have to fly directly over the road, but I did stay within gliding distance. It's always important for pilots to keep an eye out for a safe place for an emergency landing. A variety of things can go wrong while flying, and being prepared for the unexpected saves lives. I cut corners if I could see the road ahead and could make it if I had an engine failure. Each plane has a calculation in its handbook as to how far you can fly with a given amount of altitude without an operating engine.

There are reporting points in Canada when following the Alcan Highway that were indicated on the aviation chart. It was necessary to call in to report. At each airport of intended landing, there was a Flight Service office where limited weather information was available. The weather in the passes could be seen, as each office had displays showing the weather web cams around the area. However, there was no forecast. It just wasn't available. There were no guarantees of what would happen in two hours when we arrived in any one of those passes. The Alcan Highway was there for us to use in those situations.

Flying directly over the mountains is discouraged due to the remoteness of the area and lack of safe emergency landing options. Following the highway was safe because it was perfectly legal to land on the road if it was needed. I was glad it was never necessary for me to land on the road.

Having a flight plan was mandatory, but all my flights up to that point were in a straight line from point A to point B. I had no idea how I would know how long those flights would take following a road. It turned out not to be a problem because the Flight Service people knew just how long it would take me to fly that route. That problem was solved much more easily than I had expected.

When I flew a planned route, I wanted to get there and not dilly-dally for lunch. I wanted to keep going. At breakfast, I ordered lunch and took it with me. I also ate lots and lots of carrots. They gave me the natural sugar I wanted and good roughage. Staying hydrated was also important, and it didn't take long to realize I was more comfortable drinking water an hour before an intended fuel stop and not prior to the flight. Deciding on a comfortable period of time for me to fly before stopping was just as important as how long the plane could fly on its supply of fuel.

If I flew two-hour legs, I felt as if I would never get there. The flight was 1,800 nautical miles from Auburn, Maine, to Cut Bank, Montana, which was only halfway. Approximately 3,600 miles was a long way to fly from Maine to Alaska.

The FAA requires a minimum of 30 minutes of fuel when you arrive in good weather. The stress of pushing my luck to the limit made me too uncomfortable. What if the airport was closed due an unforeseen circumstance? What if there were stronger headwinds than I planned on for the flight? What if the airport was out of fuel and there wasn't enough fuel in my plane to fly to another airport? Nope, three and a half hours was it. Fortunately, there were airports spaced far enough apart to meet those needs. Passing up one was not an option since the nearest one on the route through Canada was 250 miles away and an additional two hours of flight time. This is similar to bathroom stops while driving in the car.

Jim and I settled into a nice rhythm of flying together. I flew for two days and then he flew for two. We both really wanted to fly, but after two days, we were tired and willing to give the controls over to the other person.

One day, we did have to stop due to thunderstorms in North Dakota. I was watching the radar on the navigation screen but knew there was a five-minute delay with that report. I used the Airport Directory to find the frequency I needed for the next airport to call Flight Service.

"Flight Service, N736NH on 122.2," and waited. They have several frequencies that they handle, and it was our job to let them know which one we were broadcasting on.

"736H, what is your request?"

"We are 25 miles northeast of Garrison (DO5), destination Glasgow (GGW) and I see storms approaching our route. (All airports have a three-letter designated identifier.) Will we have time to pass? I don't know how fast those storms are moving."

"Yes, you should be just fine, but stay with me on this frequency."

I did.

A few minutes later: "736NH, you are clear to pass New Town, North Dakota."

Jim was flying, and I had all the details I needed for the closest airport right on my lap just in case there was a need to land. I moved on to the next airport: Williston (XWA). We flew on.

"736NH, land and land right now. The thunderstorms contain hail and are moving faster. You will not be able to continue on your course."

"Jim, the airport is three miles to our southwest and there are two runways. I'll get the weather and see which one we should use." He turned toward the airport, and I changed the frequency on the radio to get the weather. Using the wind direction, I decided which runway to use, and relayed the information to Jim.

"Use runway one four. The winds are coming from 140 at 28, gusting to 39 (velocity of the wind in knots)." 140 is a magnetic heading.

We could see the black sky further southwest and wanted to get on the ground to secure the plane. We didn't want it damaged by hail. After landing, we found there was no room in any of the airport's hangars, and we just had to hope for the best. We took a taxi into town for lunch. While sitting there sadly looking out the restaurant window, I watched the rain come pouring down with the predicted small hail. When we arrived back at the airport, we discovered that the storm had split into a V and passed by the whole airport, saving potential hail damage to the multiple planes on the field. Hail creates hundreds of dents on a plane and reduces its value dramatically. We continued on our way safe and sound with the plane in the same condition as when we arrived.

After crossing the border at Cut Bank, Montana, and clearing customs in Lethbridge, we arrived in Red Deer, Alberta, Canada. When I walked up to the FSS office and spoke to a Flight Service representative to prepare for the flight from Red Deer to Grande Prairie, Alberta, I expressed my concern about snow showers to the west of our route that were visibly ominous.

The Flight Service man sitting in front of his computer said, "These snow showers should continue to be west of your route for about ten miles and won't be an issue after that." With that, we decided to depart.

While flying, we couldn't see a thing to the left, but it was clear as a bell with blue skies to our right. However, there was no place to safely land. There were multiple dirt roads, but I didn't see any semblance of a town, or even a house, anywhere. Instead of ten miles, which would have taken us less than ten minutes, we were still in that situation for an hour. Along with the stress of the unknown on our first trip to such a remote location and the current weather, I was getting worried about what it would be like trying to fly in the mountains. The level of stress on that first trip was high—high enough for me to be exhausted at night and sleep soundly.

Fortunately, the rest of the trip was uneventful. I thoroughly enjoyed the snow-capped mountains west of our route after the first hour. Once we started traveling through those majestic towering formations, I was ecstatic. The feeling of following a highway, flying around and through passes, and coming upon glacier-fed lakes that were a magnificent color blue was the most exciting flying I ever experienced.

The first glacier was melting into a river that flowed into Muncho Lake. The color from the glacier created blue water not unlike the Caribbean. It was spectacular to see. After that, there were more glaciers, but in each subsequent trip, it was obvious the glaciers were quickly receding due to warmer weather.

We then came through a pass and turned around a tight corner and saw Whitehorse, Yukon, Canada. It was the first large city, and the airport had two long runways. The airport sat up on a plateau with the city below along the Yukon River. I could just imagine what it was like during the Gold Rush in the 1800s.

The paddleboat that had taken fortune-seekers to Dawson was still there. However, prior to Whitehorse, many hopeful people lost their horses— which were not suited for travel over the mountains—and their own lives, too. They walked over mountains for more than 100 miles from the harbor of Skagway. A railroad was eventually built, but hundreds traveled on foot prior to that. I felt fortunate I was able to travel by air so comfortably. I enjoyed staying in Whitehorse surrounded by so much history.

When we arrived at the Alaska Airmen's trade show, we wanted to meet Charlie Center. He was the guru of the Piper Super Cruiser, the planes I flew most often. The other stop was with Landis Skis, which were the preferred ski for us to use on our planes during the winter. A tall official-looking man was taking tickets at the door. We asked where we could find Charlie.

"Just look for the guy in the overalls with a ponytail, and that's Charlie."

We finally found him outside where some of the planes were displayed. The first thing Charlie wanted to do was to sell Jim his most recent remodeled 1947 Piper Super Cruiser. Of course, that was why Charlie had brought it to the Expo. It was a beautiful yellow plane with blue striping and had all the most recent upgrades that were available, including the new left-hand door. This model Piper originally only had one door on the right. Having this other option would make it easier getting to a dock when on floats if the wind prevented you from going the other way. I was an awkward duck trying to get in that left-hand side when I was so comfortable normally sliding into the right in my school planes at home. Charlie's PA-12 was beautiful, but too expensive to be used in a flight school. I'm not sure if it was sold at the show, but I know we didn't buy it.

Since meeting Charlie, when I have any questions about that model, Charlie answers his phone and willingly helps me. When he developed a new item to test for making quick turns on the water (normally a tricky thing to do), he sent me a set to try and review for him. My seaplane season starts earlier in Maine than it does in Alaska. The "wings" were very effective in making very tight turns with great stability, and I wrote my comments for him to use. I felt respected to have been asked by Charlie to do this.

In 2020, Charlie called me to tell me about an original Super Cruiser he had remodeled and now had for sale.

"Charlie, could you send me some pictures and the specifications?"

He said, "You should remember it. It's the one you climbed into at the Expo in 2005."

I was startled that he could remember that detail.

My Second Trip

Many of our friends were pilots, and several said, "If you ever fly to Alaska again, I would like to join you."

We hadn't planned on flying there again, but the thought of that possibility was one we couldn't resist. So, on our second trip in 2007, there were three other pilots who joined me in their own airplanes. They were all competent pilots and just wanted a little added information that I could provide. I flew by myself, and Jim joined us in Alaska, as he had bronchitis and could not come with us on the long cross-country flight.

I flew so many hours doing scenic flights from 1997 to 2000 and then as a flight instructor all summer that flying by myself was a treat. I always did all the flight planning anyway, so being alone was not a problem. I relaxed listening to the hum of the engine and taking in the scenery: farm after farm out west, and northwest until reaching Fort Nelson in British Columbia, where we flew through the majestic mountains.

But it was on our way to the Fort Nelson Airport where I experienced the most frightening time I've ever had in an airplane.

We started the day at North Peace Airport in Fort St. John, British Columbia.

When getting a briefing at six a.m., I was told the weather had been the same for several days and clear below 1,500 feet, with a slight drizzle that didn't disrupt the visibility. We departed Fort St. John and within ten minutes, I was in trouble.

It's as if someone had wrapped me in a blanket of fog. At the same time, the GPS was blasting and flashing, drawing my attention to it. It repeatedly said, "PULL UP! PULL UP! TERRAIN! TERRAIN! PULL UP! PULL UP!"

"The rest of you turn around and go back to Fort St. John. The weather has changed," I broadcast on the frequency we were using.

Prior to being enveloped by the fog, I had noticed towers on top of the mountains on both sides of the Alcan Highway. The road was snaking through a narrow area of low mountains. Right now, any mountain was too high when I didn't know where I was in relation to them. I couldn't see a thing, but I had to climb if I was going to have any chance of surviving.

The GPS was useless to me with a big red flashing screen instead of showing me the road. I was unintentionally turning and had no idea where the mountains were on either side.

Straighten out, Mary, and climb! I told myself.

"St. Christopher," I prayed in earnest, "please help me to fly safely and keep the others out of harm's way."

I kept trying to clear the screen so I could tell where I was, but found that was impossible to do while flying the plane at the same time. I didn't dare turn around with all the obstacles and the other three planes right behind me. I couldn't believe I was going to die like that. I was terrified.

"Flight Service, I need to file IFR (Instrument Flight rules) to get out of this weather."

"Climb to 10,000," the briefer directed me, along with a heading to follow.

Then I started to pick up ice as I climbed through 9,000 feet. Checking the charts, I could see the minimum safe altitude (MSA) was 8,000 feet if I was in visual conditions, but lower than my assigned altitude.

"You have to stay at that altitude for radar to pick you up," I was told sternly.

"I am not equipped for icing conditions, and I'm going down to 8,000," I replied.

For five-minute intervals after that he asked, "What are your coordinates?"

I knew he was asking me about where I was to make sure that if I went down, they could find me. Just the thought of going down in this uninhabited mountainous area was terrifying. I couldn't see anything except dense fog out the window, so I concentrated on the instruments to make sure I stayed upright and on course.

I listened to the weather at Fort Nelson on my other radio, and it was clear below 12,000 feet. At that point, I opted to continue IFR to the airport at Fort Nelson instead of turning around back to Fort St. John. If I made it out alive and the weather continued the next day, I didn't want to leave Fort St. John and go through that situation again.

The closer I got to Fort Nelson, the clouds below me disappeared. The mountains off to the west were covered with snow. There was not a road, house, or airport in sight. There were, however, dirt roads for people to tend to the oil or gas wells—not much help for me.

I got through that mess safely. I was on the ground in Fort Nelson, and the others had landed safely back in Fort St. John. When I called to cancel my flight plan and tell the briefer I had landed safely, he said, "I am so sorry that happened to you today. We were all caught by surprise when the moisture dumped into the valley. That must have been terrible for you."

"It was frightening, but thanks for your guidance during my flight. I'm safely on the ground now, and that's all that matters."

Thank you, dear Lord and St. Christopher. It was not my time to die.

Once we got to Fort Nelson, things got much better. Many of the surrounding mountains were snow-capped, making the route like a fairy-land to fly through. The sky was dark blue with small puffy white cumulous clouds. This was a view any pilot would dream of.

When I wasn't busy with navigating or communicating on the radio, I enjoyed the peaceful joy of flying. I was above all the chaos of traffic on the ground. Troubles were out of my mind as I was concentrating on the surrounding beauty. I relaxed in the mesmerizing hum of the engine and beautiful scenery of farms, winding roads, and snow-capped mountains. Every time I fly, I silently express my gratitude that I can fly and think about how it has improved my self-confidence and self-worth. I have a lot to be grateful for.

On another day flying with those pilots, one of the passes between exceptionally high mountains had a rain shower in it, making it impossible to fly through. In May, going through any moisture that far north would create ice, and none of us had icing prevention on our planes. Ice adds unwanted weight, changes the dynamics of the wings, and pilots become test pilots. Picking up any amount of ice can be deadly. I looked at my aviation chart and decided to fly up a canyon to see if I could get over the top.

"Would you all please circle here, and I'll go and take a look to see if we can get on the other side of this shower?" I said to them over the radio.

I flew to the right and realized I was flying into a narrow canyon where I would not be able to turn around. I also could not get over the high ridge to continue with the others. Just as I was about to turn in an area where I did have room, one of the other pilots said he was right behind me. This was a careless thing for him to do, but there he was.

"Okay. I'm going as far as I can to the mountain on the right and then do a sharp turn to the left. Keep me in sight and stay behind me."

"Okay."

When I reached the others, he was following me, and we joined the circling pilots waiting out the showers. We circled for about 15 minutes longer and the showers continued gliding out of the way, giving us free passage so we were able to continue our flight.

When we reached Whitehorse, one of the pilots said, "Okay. I'm done for the day. I can't go on for another flight." It was only our second leg, and we normally flew three legs a day (250 miles each). That made seven hours of flying, but it was actually ten hours, including the fuel stops that were far from restful.

"That's fine, but there's a low weather system sitting off the coast that I've been watching for the last four days. If we don't continue now, we may be stuck here for several days."

"I don't care. I'm too tired to go on," he said.

I forgot how exhausting the first flight in that terrain can be, but pushing him would be dangerous, so we stayed. We did our laundry, ate in several restaurants, and stayed for three days.

On the third day at breakfast, he said, "Okay, I've rented a car and we're going to Skagway for the day. It's about a two-and-a-half-hour drive, but it's where the gold diggers frequently came by boat and walked to Whitehorse. It looks like it will be an interesting visit."

He was feeling guilty, but that was not necessary. It was just the way general aviation is. We are always restricted by the weather and sometimes you just must wait it out. That low had moved in, and we were stuck.

My Third Trip

On my third trip to Anchorage in 2008, I was flying to a conference for the Ninety-Nines, the International Organization of Women Pilots. At that time, I was a member of the Katahdin Wings Chapter in Maine. I flew with one 99 pilot who planned to fly home commercially to get back in time for work. When we reached Lethbridge, Canada, two other 99 pilots flew along with us in their planes. They wanted to fly with someone who was more experienced than they were on a trip to Alaska, and I offered to fly with them.

On the flight home, Denise Waters, another member of the 99s, who flew to the meeting commercially, flew home with me in my plane as far as Rochester, NY. I flew the rest of the way by myself.

As I mentioned before, I never made hotel arrangements ahead of time. With the required tent and sleeping bag needed for an emergency, I knew I would never be left out in the cold. After we fueled the planes in Whitehorse, the attendants at the airport's fixed base operation told us the city was full and there were no hotel rooms available. However, they, like most of the remote airports along that route, had rooms for pilots. The rooms, which in some airports only contain a bed, make it easier for pilots to make the decision to stay instead of continuing on in poor weather, or simply just because they are too tired to go on.

We were told, "If the key is in the door, the room is yours."

Denise and I didn't hesitate another moment and walked up the stairs hoping to find an available room. There was a key in one door. There was one double bed on the left. Denise and I looked at each other and decided we would just have to deal with sleeping in the same bed. I didn't know her very well, but we needed to sleep. The option of sleeping on the floor was less appealing than sharing a bed. I was tired after a busy day of flying and fell asleep quickly.

After crossing the border into the Lower 48, we stopped at Cut Bank, Montana, to clear customs and stay the night, again at the airport. This airport's pilot accommodations were larger than most with a large social area, two bedrooms, one bathroom, and a huge kitchen. We wanted to "rough it" for a change and moved in.

The next morning, there were several pilots asking questions about these women who stayed at the terminal. They wanted to know all about the route we took flying from Anchorage.

One man, as he leaned over and carefully studied the chart I showed him, was amazed that women could do such a flight. As he was pointing to the route, he said, "Well look, there aren't even any houses along that route." He looked up at me dumbfounded, expecting to find some reason we would do such a thing.

"Yes, that's right," I said.

It turned out that none of those pilots would dare to make such a flight. Denise and I have gotten many miles out of that little story for years.

In each of those trips, it consistently took 31 hours of flying to get from Maine to Anchorage, Alaska, and 30 hours to return home. Those hours were flown in either five or six days. Each flight was in our Cessna 172 XP with good avionics, a 220-horsepower engine, and an autopilot. I could fly hands-free to read a chart, eat, or just enjoy the beautiful scenery.

MY FOURTH TRIP

My fourth trip to Alaska was after heart surgery when I needed to fly 60 hours in a year to keep my FAA Designated Pilot position. I had been out of commission for several months. When I was finally cleared by the FAA to fly again, I tried flying around Maine to build time, but after five hours of that, I decided I might as well go to Alaska, and that would give me the 60 hours I needed. I didn't have that same plane any longer. I owned a Piper Super Cruiser with a 180-hp engine. The instrument panel was great since I had upgraded it, but there was no autopilot. I planned to fly alone and cherish the flight by myself.

But then I got a request I didn't expect. My neighbor Jeannie said, "Can I go with you?"

Her husband, Pete, said, "You can't ask her that."

"Why not? How would she know I want to go?"

I said, "Sure. The company would be great."

I do enjoy having passengers with me who really want to be there. During that trip, I took care of all the flight arrangements, and Jeannie planned the hotel and car reservations from the backseat prior to landing using her iPad. She also chose where to eat each night and did all the driving. This turned out to be a very workable solution. We both had our designated jobs and enjoyed them.

On the way home, Jeannie said, "I've enjoyed being part of the planning and think I need a job when I get home. This has been fun." She wanted to be home for Father's Day and took a commercial flight from Rochester, N.Y., and I flew home enjoying the peacefulness of flying alone.

We flew in May, just like the first two trips, but this time the weather was the worst from start to finish. Storm after storm steamrolled across the country, and we spent many days in towns we never expected to tour. The best one was Sault Ste. Marie, where we could see the enormous ships pass through the locks from Lake Huron to Lake Superior.

Our first stop was at the Oswego County Airport (FZY), where we spent several nights due to weather. We stayed in a hotel on the Oswego Canal. The canal was opened in 1828, is 12.7 miles long, and connects the Erie Canal at Three Rivers to Lake Ontario at Oswego. There are seven locks spanning the 118-foot change in elevation.

On one of our walks about town, we chatted with a young woman who was running a kayak operation. When she heard we were traveling to Alaska and that I was a pilot, she was fascinated. It was a cool cloudy day, so there were no visitors looking to rent a kayak.

When our conversation was over, she said, "You've made my day. I've been thinking about running for an office in town, and now you've convinced me to go for it."

There's something about being a pilot that fascinates people in general. I don't see it as being different from learning any skill that requires a license, but others do. What's fun for me is seeing people influenced by my story and then going after their own goals—which are not necessarily anything about flying an airplane.

To eliminate flying over the vast water of Lake Ontario, I flew west to Hamilton and then followed the shore to our destination airport, the Toronto/Bishop (CYTZ) airport. We cleared customs there. That airport is one of my favorites along the way. It is on an island, and the approach to it is over the water with a beautiful view of the shoreline. When leaving, and for safety, I flew over the islands to Sault Ste. Marie to clear customs again back into the U.S.

The next airport that I love to fly into is Sky Harbor (DYT) in Duluth, Minnesota. Again, this airport is on an island on the western shore of Lake Superior. There is a seaplane base there, too, with an assortment of seaplanes in hangars and on the ramp.

When landing in Dickinson, North Dakota, another plane pulled in right behind us at the fuel pump. A tall young man climbed out waiting his turn to fuel his plane. "Aren't you Mary Build, the seaplane pilot from Maine?" he said.

Very surprised and pleased, I said, "Yes, I am, but how did you know?"

"You have a belt on that I'm familiar with that you designed, and you're flying a Super Cruiser. Another pilot has that same belt and told me about you."

It thrills me to be recognized in so many places across the country. The belt has one of my planes stitched on it.

This is how it was developed: I was flying the plane when my daughter took the picture from another plane. One of the members of Katahdin Wings designed the artwork for the belt manufacturer. I sold them at the seaplane base. Seaplane pilots love to have a belt that tells everyone they're a seaplane enthusiast.

After flying through Canada, I planned on clearing customs in Northway, Alaska, as I usually did, but the customs agent, a growly sort of man, said he didn't want to make the two-hour drive again that day and we would have to clear at Anchorage. I hadn't planned for that and ended up scrambling to find out where I should fly in order to approach the airport correctly. At the same time, the air traffic controller in Anchorage was very busy and really didn't need someone unaware of the area flying into his busy airport. I ended up in my little two-seater slowly descending into a huge international airport while four enormous 747s were waiting for departure.

I never felt so small in my life. The Anchorage International Airport was so huge that after I landed, I couldn't see where I needed to go. All the signage was for pilots who were way up in the air while they taxied their planes, and I was crawling. I had to ask for help, which I hate to do. The controller was more than happy to give me directions to make sure I didn't go astray on his busy field.

While we were in Anchorage, we drove to Talkeetna and took a scenic flight to Denali (Mt. McKinley) in a bright red de Havilland Otter with other passengers. We were given big rubber boots to go over our shoes and climbed aboard.

The pilot announced as he climbed in, "The mountain received two feet of snow last night, and we may be able to land up there if the weather holds up."

It is not unusual for Denali to develop its own weather, and it seldom stays in the clear all day. That day, we were fortunate enough to fly all around that towering mountain and land on a freshly snow-covered glacier. I couldn't believe how lucky we were to have such a crystal-clear day to fly. The landing was smooth on the new carpet of snow. The pilot circled around facing the departure run downhill prior to stopping and letting the skis dig into the plush carpet.

While dressed in one light shirt over another and our big rubber boots, we climbed out of the big red plane at over 7,000 feet. I was concerned we might be cold at that altitude, but the sun warmed my back and my face. It was so bright, I was glad I had on sunglasses. We took lots of pictures of that red plane against the pure bright-white snow topped with clear blue skies. It is one of many experiences on my trips to Alaska that I will never forget.

That last trip to and from Maine took 99 hours of flying. First of all, I was much slower. Instead of the 120 knots (138 mph) I enjoyed in the Cessna 172 XP, this Super Cruiser flew at 91 knots (105) mph. With no headwind, the trip would have taken 40 hours. Instead, it took almost 50. I experienced a headwind all the way to Anchorage and most of the way home. That was a very long trip and took three weeks of flying.

2017 Route from Maine to Anchorage

Jeannie and Mary beside the de Havilland Otter on a glacier on Denali

Glacier flying to Denali

Sky Harbor Airport in Duluth, Minnesota

Spectacular section of the Alcan Highway we followed

PRIVACY ACT STATEMENT: This statement is provided pursuant to the Privacy Act of 1974, 5 USC § 552a. The authority for collecting this information is contained in 49 U.S.C. §§ 40113, 44702, 44703, 44709, and 14 C.F.R. Part 6 - (Part 61, 63, 65, or 67. The principal purpose for which the information is intended to be used is to allow you to submit your flight plan. Submission of the data is voluntary. Failure to provide all required information may result in you not being able to submit your flight plan. The information collected on this form will be included in a Privacy Act System of Records known as DOT/FAA 847, titled 'Aviation Records on Individuals' and will be subject to the routine uses published in the System of Records Notice (SORN) for DOT/FAA 847 (see www.dot.gov/privacy/privacyactnotices).

Paperwork Reduction Act Statement: A federal agency may not conduct or sponsor, and a person is not required to respond to, nor shall a person be subject to a penalty for failure to comply with a collection of information subject to the requirements of the Paperwork Reduction Act unless that collection of information displays a current valid OMB Control Number. The OMB Control Number for this information collection is 2120-0026. Public reporting for this collection of information is estimated to be approximately 2.5 minutes per response, including the time for reviewing instructions,completing and reviewing the collection of information. All responses to this collection of information are mandatory per 14 CFR Part 91. Comments concerning the accuracy of this burden and suggestions for reducing the burden should be directed to the FAA at: 800 Independence Ave. SW, Washington, DC 20591, Attn: Information Collection Clearance Officer, ASP-110.

Form Approved: OMB No. 2120-0026 Exp. 7/31/2023

FLIGHT PLAN U.S. DEPARTMENT OF TRANSPORTATION FEDERAL AVIATION ADMINISTRATION	(FAA USE ONLY) ☐ PILOT BRIEFING ☐ STOPOVER	☐ VNR	TIME STARTED	SPECIALIST INITIALS

| 1. TYPE VFR / IFR / DVFR | 2. AIRCRAFT IDENTIFICATION | 3. AIRCRAFT TYPE / SPECIAL EQUIPMENT | 4. TRUE AIRSPEED KTS | 5. DEPARTURE POINT | 6. DEPARTURE TIME PROPOSED (Z) / ACTUAL (Z) | 7. CRUISING ALTITUDE |

8. ROUTE OF FLIGHT

| 9. DESTINATION (Name of airport and city) | 10. EST. TIME ENROUTE HOURS / MINUTES | 11. REMARKS |

| 12. FUEL ON BOARD HOURS / MINUTES | 13. ALTERNATE AIRPORT(S) | 14. PILOT'S NAME, ADDRESS & TELEPHONE NUMBER & AIRCRAFT HOME BASE | 15. NUMBER ABOARD |
| | | 17. DESTINATION CONTACT/TELEPHONE (OPTIONAL) | |

16. COLOR OF AIRCRAFT

CIVIL AIRCRAFT PILOTS. FAR Part 91 requires you file an IFR flight plan to operate under instrument flight rules in controlled airspace. Failure to file could result in a civil penalty not to exceed $1,000 for each violation (Section 901 of the Federal Aviation Act of 1958, as amended). Filing of a VFR flight plan is recommended as a good operating practice. See also Part 99 for requirements concerning DVFR flight plans.

FAA Form 7233-1 (8-82)
Electronic Version (Adobe)

CLOSE VFR FLIGHT PLAN WITH _____ FSS ON ARRIVAL

MILITARY STOPOVER (FAA USE ONLY)

| TYPE ☐ IFR ☐ VFR | AIRCRAFT IDENTIFICATION | AIRCRAFT TYPE/SPECIAL EQUIPMENT | REMARKS |
| DEPARTURE POINT | DESTINATION | ETA | |

TAS	DEP. PT	ETD	ALTITUDE	ROUTE OF FLIGHT	DESTINATION	ETE	REMARKS
KTS							
KTS							
KTS							
KTS							
REMARKS							INITIALS

FAA Form 7233-1 (8-82)   Electronic Version (Adobe)

US Flight Plan Form

NAV CANADA CANADIAN FLIGHT PLAN AND FLIGHT ITINERARY / PLAN DE VOL ET ITINÉRAIRE DE VOL CANADIEN   ICAO FLIGHT PLAN / PLAN DE VOL OACI

PRIORITY / PRIORITÉ   ADDRESSEE(S) / DESTINATAIRE(S)

<< ≡ FF →   << ≡

FILING TIME / HEURE DE DÉPÔT   ORIGINATOR / EXPÉDITEUR → << ≡

SPECIFIC IDENTIFICATION OF ADDRESSEE(S) AND/OR ORIGINATOR / IDENTIFICATION PRÉCISE DU(DES) DESTINATAIRE(S) ET/OU DE L'EXPÉDITEUR

3 MESSAGE TYPE / TYPE DE MESSAGE   7 AIRCRAFT IDENTIFICATION / IDENTIFICATION DE L'AÉRONEF   8 FLIGHT RULES / RÈGLES DE VOL   TYPE OF FLIGHT / TYPE DE VOL

<< ≡ (FPL   –   <<

9 NUMBER / NOMBRE   TYPE OF AIRCRAFT / TYPE D'AÉRONEF   WAKE TURBULENCE CAT. / CAT. DE TURBULENCE DE SILLAGE   10 EQUIPMENT / ÉQUIPEMENT

–   /   –   << ≡

13 DEPARTURE AERODROME / AÉRODROME DE DÉPART   TIME / HEURE   –   << ≡

15 CRUISING SPEED / VITESSE DE CROISIÈRE   ALTITUDE / LEVEL / NIVEAU   ROUTE / ROUTE

– 0 0 0 0 0   0 0 0 0 0 →   << ≡

16 DESTINATION AERODROME / AÉRODROME DE DESTINATION   TOTAL EET / DURÉE TOTALE ESTIMÉE DAYS/JOURS HRS MINS   SAR HRS MINS   ALTN AERODROME / AÉRODROME DE DÉGAGEMENT   2ND ALTN AERODROME / 2e AÉRODROME DE DÉGAGEMENT

–   →   →   << ≡

18 OTHER INFORMATION / RENSEIGNEMENTS DIVERS
–

)<< ≡

19 ENDURANCE / AUTONOMIE   EMERGENCY RADIO / RADIO DE SECOURS

HRS MINS   PERSONS ON BOARD / PERSONNES À BORD   UHF   VHF   ELT   ELT TYPE / TYPE D'ELT

– E /   →P /   →R/ U   V   E

SURVIVAL EQUIPMENT / ÉQUIPEMENT DE SURVIE   JACKETS / GILETS DE SAUVETAGE

POLAR / POLAIRE   DESERT / DÉSERT   MARITIME / MARITIME   JUNGLE / JUNGLE   LIGHT / LAMPES   FLUORES / FLUORES   UHF   VHF

→ S / P   D   M   J   →J / L   F   U   V

DINGHIES / CANOTS

NUMBER / NOMBRE   CAPACITY / CAPACITÉ   COVER / COUVERTURE   COLOUR / COULEUR

→ D /   →   C →   << ≡   WHEELS / ROUES ☐   SEAPLANE / HYDRAVION ☐   SKIS ☐   AMPHIBIAN / AMPHIBIE ☐

AIRCRAFT COLOUR AND MARKINGS / COULEUR ET MARQUES DE L'AÉRONEF

A /

REMARKS / REMARQUES

→ N /   << ≡

AN ARRIVAL REPORT WILL BE FILED WITH / UN COMPTE RENDU D'ARRIVÉE SERA NOTIFIÉ À :

NAME AND PHONE NUMBER OR ADDRESS OF PERSONS(S) OR COMPANY TO BE NOTIFIED IF SEARCH AND RESCUE ACTION INITIATED / NOM ET NUMÉRO DE TÉLÉPHONE OU ADRESSE DE LA (DES) PERSONNE(S) OU COMPAGNIE À AVISER SI DES RECHERCHES SONT ENTREPRISES

PILOT-IN-COMMAND / PILOTE COMMANDANT DE BORD   PILOT'S LICENCE NO. / N° DE LICENCE DU PILOTE

C /   )<< ≡

FILED BY / DÉPOSÉ PAR   SPACE RESERVED FOR ADDITIONAL REQUIREMENTS / ESPACE RÉSERVÉ À DES FINS SUPPLÉMENTAIRES

NAVCAN26-0516 (2010-01)

NAV Canada Flight Plan Form

Alaskan Survival Kit Regulations

Alaska state law (AS 02.35.110. Emergency Rations and Equipment) was modified a while back to reduce the equipment required to be carried. The current regulations require that no airman may make a flight inside the state with an aircraft unless the following emergency equipment is carried:

1. The minimum equipment to be carried during summer months is as follows (for all single-engine and for multiengine aircraft licensed to carry 15 passengers or less):
     (A) rations for each occupant sufficient to sustain life for one week
     (B) one axe or hatchet
     (C) one first aid kit
     (D) an assortment of tackle such as hooks, flies, lines, and sinkers
     (E) one knife
     (F) fire starter
     (G) one mosquito head net for each occupant
     (H) two small signaling devices such as colored smoke bombs, railroad fuses, or Very pistol shells, in sealed metal containers

2. In addition to the above, the following must be carried as minimum equipment from October 15 to April 1 of each year:
     (A) one pair of snowshoes
     (B) one sleeping bag
     (C) one wool blanket for each occupant over four

As you can see, the Alaskan regulations are minimal and do not address much in the way of specifics or quality. The old regulations were similarly minimal, but required double the food, a gill net, and a firearm, and specified matches instead of a generic "firestarter." The old requirements were as follows:

1. The minimum equipment to be carried during summer months is as follows (for all single-engine and for multiengine aircraft licensed to carry 15 passengers or less):

a. food for each occupant sufficient to sustain life for two weeks

b. one axe or hatchet

c. one first aid kit

d. one pistol, revolver, shotgun, or rifle and ammunition for same

e. one small gill net and an assortment of tackle such as hooks, flies, lines, sinkers, etc.

f. one knife

g. two small boxes of matches

h. one mosquito head net for each occupant

i. two small signaling devices such as colored smoke bombs, railroad fuses, or Very pistol shells, in sealed metal containers

2. In addition to the above, the following must be carried as minimum equipment from October 15 to April 1 of each year:

a. one pair of snowshoes

b. one sleeping bag

c. one wool blanket for each occupant over four

Canadian Survival Kit Regulations

Canada used to have pretty stringent regulations regarding required survival gear. Then they revised the regulations, leaving the contents virtually undefined and ambiguous, presenting unscrupulous operators with loopholes large enough to fly a 747 through. The current version of the regulations follows, with the former version—a fairly good guide for what may be considered acceptable with modification by some government field personnel—following the current regulations.

Survival Equipment—Flights over Land

602.61 (1) Subject to subsection (2), no person shall operate an aircraft over land unless there is carried on board survival equipment, sufficient for the survival on the ground of each person on board, given the geographical area, the season of the year, and anticipated seasonal climatic variations, that provides the means for

(a) starting a fire,

(b) providing shelter,

(c) providing or purifying water, and

(d) visually signaling distress.

(2) Subsection (1) does not apply in respect of

(a) a balloon, a glider, a hang glider, a gyroplane, or an ultra-light aeroplane;

(b) an aircraft that is operated within 25 nautical miles of the aerodrome of departure and that has the capability of radio communication with surface-based radio station for the duration of the flight;

(c) a multi-engine aircraft that is operated south of 66 30' north latitude

(i) in IFR flight within controlled airspace, or

(ii) along designated air routes.

(d) an aircraft that is operated by an air operator, where the aircraft is equipped with equipment specified in the air operator's company operations manual, but not with the equipment required by subsection (1); or

(e) an aircraft that is operated in a geographical area where and at a time of year when the survival of the persons on board is not jeopardized.

AIR RACE CLASSIC 2006

"I can do this, Jenny! I'm finally starting to feel better, and sure, I'll be able to fly in June."

"Great!" Jenny Jorgensen said enthusiastically. "I was afraid you couldn't make it this year."

At that time, I had been in the seaplane business for nine years. When I first started in 1997, Jenny, a friend and fellow woman pilot, used to come to the seaplane base and talk to customers while I was doing scenic flights. With no notice, she simply showed up every Wednesday, and we really had fun working together for the day.

The year after my first flight to Alaska in 2006, I couldn't fly, drive, or even walk comfortably around the house, so my right hip was replaced. It was February and a year since my left hip had been replaced. My recovery was taking longer than the previous surgery. Jenny and I had talked about the possibility of racing in an upcoming all-women's air race, but I wasn't sure I was going to recover in time.

Jenny was the only woman pilot friend I could think of to fly as my copilot. She came to visit just prior to the sign-up deadline for the Air Race Classic. This race goes back to the Powder Puff Derby, the first all-women's air race, and is the epicenter of women's air racing.

Pilots range in age from 17 to 90 years old and include everything from students, teachers, doctors, airline pilots, business owners, and professionals, to air traffic controllers. Each race team, consisting of at least two women pilots, must fly VFR during daylight hours only and are given four days to make fly-bys at each of the eight or nine timing points. The race route, which changes each year, is approximately 2,400 statute miles in length. This year's race would start in Arizona and end in Michigan— and participating in the race is something I had wanted to do ever since I'd earned my pilot certificate 14 years before.

Jenny's visit, I'm sure, was to see if I was up to the race. I stayed put during most of her visit and she never brought up the race.

After she left, I gradually began feeling better. In just two weeks, I called her to let her know that—as far as I was concerned—we were going to participate in the race.

We planned to fly a Cessna 172XP that Jim and I owned. I took care of all the paperwork to get us signed up, which included sending in all the information on the plane.

The course is different each year and all pilots have to fly to the start of the race, fly the course, and then fly home. That year's race started in Mesa, Arizona, and ended in Menominee, Michigan, with us flying through New Mexico, Texas, Louisiana, Oklahoma, Kansas, and Minnesota. My home base was in Auburn, Maine, and Jenny flew out of Wiscasset.

In May, just a few weeks before we embarked on this 2,500-mile adventure, race official Denise Waters called me with bad news.

"Mary, I'm so sorry to be calling so late in this process, but your plane is not eligible for the race. All planes have to be capable of flying full power for the duration of the 2,500 miles, and yours is limited to full power for the first five minutes."

At that time, pilots did not receive the rules prior to registering for the race. I knew about the limitation of the power, but also knew I would bring the power back to the proper setting, thinking I could still race.

"The reason this is one of the rules of the race is that pilots in the past have become so involved in winning, they push their limits and have engine problems," Denise explained.

My heart dropped. I couldn't believe I was receiving that phone call.

"Jenny, you won't believe the call I just received. We can't use the XP."

"Oh no!" Jenny was just as disappointed as I.

I explained why, adding, "Let me think about this and see if I can come up with another one. We've done too much work to not go."

That led me to picking up the phone and calling Bob Wiplinger, whose company, Wipaire, is known for the manufacture of floats for general aviation aircraft and for remodeling aircraft for those floats.

"Hi, Bob, I hope all is well with you."

"It is, thanks, Mary. What can I do for you?"

"I think I have an advertising opportunity for you, Bob."

I didn't really recognize myself in that conversation. It was totally out of character for me to ask anyone for anything. I explained my dilemma about not being able to fly my plane and thought it may be of interest for him to have a plane fly in a race like this and get lots of exposure.

"Mary, let me think about this. I'll have an answer for you on Friday."

I waited until 3:45 p.m. on Friday and decided I couldn't stand it any longer. I was also afraid they might close on Friday at four p.m. instead of five, and of course, I was afraid I would be forgotten.

"Hello, Mary."

Holding my breath, I thought, Oh dear. I've made a fool of myself.

"Hi, Bob. You suggested I call you today to see if you'd decided to enter one of your planes in the Air Race."

"Oh, yes. You know, I think I would like to do this."

My chest felt like it had jumping beans in it. If I could have shouted "YIPPEE!" I would have, but it just was not an appropriate time to do so.

"Thank you, Bob. I really appreciate your doing this. The race starts on Tuesday the 23rd, and my copilot and I will be out on Monday the 12th. Is that okay with you?"

"Sure, Mary. That will be fine. I have a Cessna 182 on amphibious floats for you."

"Thank you, Bob. That will be perfect," I said.

I had no idea if the race would allow this plane. With fingers crossed, I called Denise again.

"Denise, do you think this replacement will work?" I asked as I gave her all the details about the new plane.

"I'll look and see and get right back to you."

I'm guessing she didn't know any more than I did, but she agreed to check it out. I also thought she wanted to hang up quickly before she laughed at me. I thought it was crazy to enter a race with floats on that would add extra weight and drag. I couldn't imagine what others would think.

It was already the third week in May, and we had to be in Mesa, Arizona, on Friday, June 16th, prior to the race for inspections, pre-race instructions, and briefings. Another week went by and Denise finally called me back.

"Hi, Mary. It looks like you're all set and can race this plane."

After thanking her, I hung up quickly, ecstatic. I couldn't wait to tell Jenny but had to wait until she got home from school. We were going to race!

On the Sunday prior to our mandatory arrival in Arizona, Jenny and I took a bus to Boston, stayed overnight, then caught an early flight to Minneapolis. We then took a taxi to the hotel in South St. Paul.

"I know this hotel is within walking distance of the airport where the plane is, so we'll walk down tomorrow morning," I explained.

"I'm so relieved to be here and more than happy to have a nice walk in the morning," she answered.

We walked up one flight of stairs to our appointed room and found the beds were not made.

"Let's see if they have another room. I'm tired and don't really want to wait for them to clean this one."

Sure enough, they did. It was about 15 minutes after we settled in the new room that I realized the race numbers for the plane, protected in their nice little cardboard tube, were missing.

"Hi. This is room 223, and we just moved in from our former room that wasn't ready, and I need to go back in there to get something I left there by mistake."

"Oh sure," said the man at the desk. "I'll be right up and open it for you."

The numbers that we carted from state to state and protected with our lives were not there. How could that have happened so fast?

"Will you please check with the maid service and see if they set them aside?" I begged.

No luck. Incredible how things can disappear from a hotel room just as if they didn't exist!

Our designated race number was 33, and the first set arrived from my printer who had followed all the guidelines. The rules specified that the numbers had to be 18" high and 3" wide to be placed on the tail for good visibility. The printer followed the dimensions but put both numbers in that 3" width. There was no way they could be read from the ground when flying by the finish line at over 100 knots and 200 feet above the ground! So I went to the printer again and explained how EACH number must be 18" high and 3" wide. Of course, it was last-minute, and they had to be rushed in order for us to meet our scheduled departure the following week. We had to have those numbers on the plane upon our arrival!

"We'll have to get them in Arizona, somehow. It took two weeks to get the first set in Maine, so this should be interesting," I said.

However, I had an airplane to think about, and the number issue was put aside until we got to Arizona.

Bob Wiplinger's crew at Wipaire was extremely helpful and willing to present the log books and other documents we had to take with us. They had to put my name on the insurance policy as per the rules for the Air Race and did so without a fuss.

They handed me the keys on Monday afternoon. No checkout in the plane? I didn't want to act as if I needed it, of course, but I had assumed someone would check me out. Good grief.

On Tuesday morning, Jenny and I walked back down the gently sloped road to the airport with our luggage in tow and embarked on our journey from South St. Paul, Minnesota, to Mesa, Arizona. I didn't know the airspace, nor did I know how to operate all the avionics in the plane. Everything was digital! I'll just have to learn on the way, I thought.

It took us two days to fly to Mesa from South St. Paul. Each night, I studied up on the manuals and had a good handle on things when we arrived.

My daughter Anna and granddaughter Brianna surprised us with their arrival from California to greet us. I was very happy to see them and proud that they'd driven all that way for support. I was afraid I would not have enough time to spend with them. We were going to be very busy attending all our preflight mandatory meetings.

"Mom, don't worry about spending time with us," Anna assured me. "We're here to cheer for you."

Due to the issue with our race numbers for the plane, I needed to find a printer willing to rush an order for us. I did, but needed to go and pick them up. We didn't have cell phones then, so I found printers in the Yellow Pages in the phone book in the hotel room.

Jenny wrote down the directions, and we hopped into Anna's Triumph TR7. It was blistering hot, but Jenny and I love convertibles, so we chose to drive with the top down. Not sure that was a smart move, but that's what we did. We picked up the numbers about a half-hour drive away and returned to the airport to apply them to the plane. So far, so good.

With all our compulsory briefings out of the way, it was race day. At the beginning of that insufferably hot day in Mesa, Jenny and I dutifully drank a pint of water before daring to go out in the heat. It was 90 degrees at eight a.m. and forecasted to go to 110 degrees by nine a.m.

With our paperwork done and our numbers glued efficiently on the side of the tail to allow timers to record our takeoff and landing, we were embarking on our first Air Race Classic.

We were close to the last to enter due to my slow recovery from my second hip replacement, but we made it. I'm the competitor of the two of us, and I was itching with anticipation to get into the waiting plane.

It was hot enough to fry an egg on the tarmac, and we were sitting in the blazing sun surrounded by windows in this mighty machine high up off the ground on amphibious floats. We had the number 33, very close to the end of the line of departing airplanes in the race. There were 35 planes that year.

Following the rules of the Air Race, we were 33rd to take off. One after another, the racers rolled down the long runway of over 5,000' and were off to do their best flying time from airport to airport. The race was 2,153.4 nautical miles that year, or 2,478.3 statute miles, and would take us either three or four days to accomplish. We had specific airports to land at, or to fly over for timing, and had to be at the terminus by Friday at sunset.

The race route that year was from Mesa, Arizona, to Santa Teresa, New Mexico; Ozona, Texas; Bryan, Texas; Bastrop, Louisiana; Ada, Oklahoma; Lawrence, Kansas; Albert Lea, Minnesota; and finally the terminus in Menominee, Michigan.

The goal was to do better than our handicap, and we could do that by choosing the best altitude with favoring winds, or even skip flying for a day for better winds. It takes skill and lots of luck to get into the Top 10. Everyone wants to win, so the competition is stiff. All those women were good pilots and lots of fun to be around.

We were all spaced by 30 seconds for takeoff, leaving us sitting on the ramp an hour and 20 minutes, including the ten minutes prior to the start when we climbed in. The race started exactly at eight a.m., and by twenty past nine, Jenny and I were soaked in sweat running down our backs that was sticking to the leather seats. We drank more water.

We sat in the plane in anxious anticipation of racing madly out of this airport and to the next one, the Dona Ana County Airport in Santa Teresa, New Mexico (5T6), 270.9 nautical miles away.

I was certain that we would get good timing during every leg. Even though I was soaking wet from sweating profusely for over an hour, I was more excited than I had ever been prior to flying. However, I had never flown with full throttle for any length of time until the day before when flying the handicap flight. All the lights on the panel kept flashing as though lightning was hitting the plane, and I was scared to death trying to figure out how I could possibly fly the race if all the avionics went out.

The main feature was, of course, the GPS giving us a nice straight line, but without that, we would be dependent on the aviation sectional chart. Jenny had dutifully marked our route with a red marker to get us there, but not anywhere near as accurately as the avionics in the plane could take us. In order to win this race, I would have to be as precise as humanly possible. In addition to accuracy, we had to follow all the rules or suffer penalty points. I, of course, had no intention of making any mistakes. At that point, I felt as invincible as a very hot Wonder Woman.

Finally, one of the race committee women walked toward us and gave us the circling arm signal to start our engine. I did that and lavishly enjoyed the taxi down the ramp to the beginning of the runway, bathing in the moving air from the propeller through the door I had left open. The okay to start was given by a different woman with gray hair, her white Air Race Classic shirt sticking to her back.

I already had plenty of time to make sure the trim was set properly, seat belts were on, and all the dozen or so items on the checklist were completed. I lined up on the runway, corrected the directional gyro (DG) to the runway heading, and pushed in the throttle to full power. The engine did not function well due to the heat, and we rolled pathetically slowly down the runway and barely reached takeoff speed before the end!

The plane could not as fly well as I'd expected it to due to the weather, and our climb out was at a ridiculously slow rate. I was sure we would come in last at that rate.

Resigned to the fact that everyone else was dealing with the same conditions, I followed the nice straight line and continued to climb toward a legal easterly altitude of 7,500'. Pilots are to fly at odd numbers plus 500' traveling east and even numbers plus 500' traveling west to keep us safely separated during flight. This rule only applies to a flying altitude 3,000' above the ground. The highest mountain on our route was 6,568', I chose 7,000' to gain more speed and forgot about climbing any higher.

After about an hour, we were peacefully flying over the mountain range with only a slight amount of turbulence when Jenny said, "Mary, I have to pee."

Good grief. "Jenny, there's no place for us to stop and we're racing."

Very slowly and quietly, Jenny said, "Mary, I have to pee."

"Well, can you try and hold it? I know another hour will be difficult, but can you?"

"Mary," Jenny said, in the same matter-of-fact way with no variance in her voice from the last time, "I have to pee."

"Well, all I have are plastic bags, Jenny. I know that's going to be difficult, but it's all we have in the plane that I can think of."

Jenny took the two Ziploc bags and squeezed through the two front seats into the back. We had taken out the back seats due to weight and balance issues. Rules said we had to have full tanks for our first takeoff, and with the heavy amphibious floats on, there was a limited amount of room for anything extra for total weight. So, at least she didn't have seats in the way. She also did not have a rug to worry about, but I thought that might make it a little hard to keep from sliding. I hoped she would manage without too much difficulty.

"Hey, Jenny!"

Silence from the uninterested copilot in the back.

I'm just overflowing with good news, so I say again to a still-ignoring-me copilot, "Guess what? We just gained two knots with you back there. When you moved, I had to move the trim to adjust to the change of center of gravity. With your weight back there, I could trim it forward, making the wings actually straighter into the wind, giving us more speed! Can you stay there?"

"NO!" said my friend. "I am NOT going to stay here!"

Oh dear. She's upset.

"Do you have any idea how hard it is to pee like that?"

I don't.

"First of all, the bags were too small. I had to stop, seal the bag, and then use the second one, not to mention sliding around on the floor during turbulence!"

Her red face showed her aggravation. I didn't dare ask if she was mad at me!

Again she squeezed into the front and got settled back into her seat with her curly hair sticking to the side of her face. I changed the trim and lost two knots. Darn!

Wait! Let's push our seats back to move the CG back again and see if that works. Yes! Two knots pop back on the digital screen. We're gaining speed again.

Jenny and I thought we had discovered something original while smiling our way to Santa Teresa, New Mexico. We were confident of doing much better than we expected after our slow and painful climb out of the Falcon Field Airport in Mesa. We were not only unaware that any plane would fly faster with the weight in the back, but we were oblivious to the consequences of this maneuver.

"Can you see the airport yet?"

"No, not yet, but it's got to be right over there," she said as she pointed toward the east.

Each airport we were to arrive at had specific race rules on how to enter the timing line, including our departure directions for takeoff. Jenny and I had been comparing notes, making sure we did everything according to the specifications. I needed to fly wings level one mile from the approach end of the runway and cross the timing line 200' above the ground. We focused on what we needed to do and made sure we knew who was going to do what in reference to communicating and timing.

Jenny set the appropriate frequency on the radio, I did the communicating, and she took care of the timing. Our time was kept to help with any discrepancies along the way with the timers. The timers used a world digital clock that matched all clocks used in the race, coordinating all records accurately.

"Are you ready with the timing?" I asked.

"Thanks. I've got it."

"You also need to be over the runway and fly straight over it. Then you have to fly to the right to cool the engine," she said.

We were discussing our first timing line.

"Jenny!...Jenny! Can you reach the rudders?"

"No! I thought you had control of the plane!"

"I did, but I don't!"

That banter was happening as I was trying to turn toward the timing line that was looming perilously ahead.

"Do you see you're about to go too fast? You're reaching the red line," said Jenny.

I had full power, air speed was at red line, meaning I could not go any faster, and we were diving toward the finish line. We were scrambling as if we had fire ants in our pants.

We were having trouble because there was nothing we could reach to hold onto and pull ourselves forward. Pulling up on the lever in front of the seat brings up the pin that is locking the seat in place. The track on the floor had several holes in it to adjust the seat correctly for the pilot and front seat passenger, in this case, the pilot's and copilot's seats.

Sliding our seats forward was a challenge. We had to loosen our seat belts to reach the V braces over the instrument panel. These extra braces are installed in a seaplane to give more support to the wings, which are apt to rock when on the water. That day, they saved us. I had been so excited about gaining two extra knots, I forgot we had let our seats go back from the controls. The autopilot had been doing its job just fine up until I needed to turn it off to fly the plane toward the timing line.

I reached for my side and Jenny reached for hers as we slid our individual seats forward close enough to reach the rudders. As we positioned ourselves where we needed to be, we released the lever in front of our seats and the locking pin dropped into place under the seat on the track. Our seats were then safely secured. I could level the plane and keep it straight just in time to cross the timing line where the timers were waiting for our arrival. We were going faster than I've ever flown a plane and it was exhilarating!

"Holy cow! This is only the first of eight legs! I've never had so much fun flying an airplane!"

I was ecstatic and turned to Jenny. Her curly blond hair, usually springy, was now pasted to her brow. She was not having fun. However, she was ready to go to the FBO and submit our fuel request. We would be one of the last ones taken care of because we were near the end of the line with our 33 race number.

NEXT LEG: THE RIO GRANDE

"DO NOT—UNDER ANY CIRCUMSTANCES—ENTER INTO MEXICO'S AIRSPACE!" said Lara of the Air Race Classic. "The Air Race Committee couldn't get permission to fly over Mexico. In addition, do not go into El Paso's airspace."

All the racers were given detailed documents with clear instructions on where to report our position while flying along the Rio Grande, the border between El Paso, Texas, and Mexico. I had so much information coming at me in such a short period of time, it felt like being sprayed with a fire hose.

"Jenny, this second leg of the race is going to be one of the easier ones for us to navigate. We'll just have to follow the Rio Grande, which will be easy to see, and then continue straight after we pass El Paso. We'll just have to be sure and report our position at each designated point as directed at one of our preflight meetings."

"I'm glad we won't have to watch our exact heading for that stretch of the river," Jenny said. "It will give me a chance to look outside and not have to be staring at our course on the GPS. In this heat, it will be a relief, since I get a little nauseous with my head looking at the instruments all the time."

When we were approaching the section of the route where we would follow the Rio Grande, I felt more comfortable. Looking at the GPS, I could see how it snaked along, separating the two airspaces we had to avoid. I was focused inside with the GPS but not looking out, making sure I didn't deviate into restricted airspace. Jenny was watching out the window for any traffic and for the Rio Grande.

I made gentle turns to stay over the river, but about one-third of the way, everything went completely blank on the instrument panel. The GPS was off. The electrical compass, all navigation, and the communication radios were off just as if they didn't exist.

"Oh, shit!" I mumbled as my heart skipped a beat.

"What?" Jenny asked, concerned. When something like that is said in a plane, a pilot is on high alert, thinking the worst is about to happen.

"Shit, shit, shit," I said, and that alarmed Jenny even more.

Then she looked at the panel and saw what I was looking at—the navigation panel that had blinked so furiously due to the heat was completely void of all digital displays. That was all the equipment I needed for the utmost accuracy flying between the very busy El Paso Airport and Mexico, and to know where we were for our reporting points. I couldn't tell where to report, nor could I report even if I did know!

I'll just look out, follow the river, and use the chart that we were given in our meeting before the race, I thought.

"Where's the Rio Grande?" I asked. I couldn't see a river of any size in front of or below us.

"I don't know," Jenny said.

"What do you mean, you don't know?" I felt like I was wrapped in a blanket of nettles. The Rio Grande should be huge with a name like that, but it was nowhere in sight. "We were over it a second ago," I said.

Jenny said, "I know, I saw it on the GPS, but never saw it on the ground."

"I wonder what the repercussions will be for invading airspace we're not supposed to be in," I said. "Look ahead and see if you can spot it."

"Mary, I can't see the river."

"Okay, then we'll just have to fly toward that curve in the ground ahead and hope it's where we need to be." I was probably in El Paso's airspace, the lesser of two evils, I thought, but they couldn't detect who we were because all our electrical transmitting equipment was off. "They'll see us on radar, but that's it."

I was doing the best I could to follow a line I couldn't see. I really expected the Rio Grande to be huge, but it appeared to be a brook and not visible from the air.

Just when I thought we are clear of El Paso, I said, "Look, Jenny!"

"Now what?"

"Everything is back on again!" Now that we were past the most critical point in that leg, all the lights on the panel were back on and not even flashing.

"How did that happen in the first place?"

"I have no idea. Overheating is my best guess."

It's not like we could pull over to the side of the road to take a break. I had to keep flying just as straight as I could to Ozona, Texas. I had no intention of staying any longer than to get more fuel and use the bathroom. I was hoping there were no officials on the ground waiting for us. I sure didn't want to get grounded over this situation. After the fiasco of not obeying any of the directions given us over the Rio Grande, arriving at Ozona and the timing line was uneventful. Nothing could compare with that fear of breaking the rules.

The worst-case scenario for me would have been to be thought of as a poor pilot by my peers. I strive to do what is right and hate when I make a mistake. When we arrived at Ozona, I expected someone to tell me, "Call the El Paso tower." But that didn't happen. I could have had a stern talking-to. If I'd created a dangerous situation, like getting in the way of an airliner, that could have ended in a suspension of my license for several months. Fortunately, nothing happened, but it sure was a frightful few minutes.

We continued the race with good communication from weather briefers, lots of luck, and good coordination between the two of us. We came in at fifth place that year just as proud as we could be.

INTERNATIONAL SEAPLANE FLY-IN

Every September, I mark off the days for the annual International Seaplane Fly-In in Greenville, Maine—always.

It's a Mecca of sorts for seaplane pilots, kicking off with a sunset cruise aboard the *Katahdin*, an old logging boat, on the Thursday after Labor Day. The weekend's festivities end Sunday morning with a Seaplane Pilot's Association breakfast, also aboard the *Katahdin*. In between those two events are a variety of activities, including several competitions for the seaplane pilots gathered at Moosehead Lake.

Since 1998, I have watched all the competitions. I wanted to compete, but didn't feel competent. I believed my skills simply did not measure up to the young men who had been flying in seaplanes since they were in diapers.

One extended family, the Dunns, lived on Beech Hill Pond, east of Bangor, and many of the family members had their own planes. Tommy and Brian were always competing for their families' bragging rights. I decided it was much more fun to watch than it was to even think about competing. So for years, I watched from shore.

One of the events they participated in was the Bushman's Canoe Race. This is how it goes:

Official says "Go" and pushes his stopwatch. The pilot taxies the plane, and the other member of the team paddles the canoe as fast as possible to the floating dock in the middle of the cove. When they both arrive, they work together to attach the canoe to the top of the float, the pilot and passenger get into the plane with the paddle and the plane is started. They taxi back to the dock as fast as possible. The propeller must be stopped before their door is opened. Once the canoe is untied and placed on the dock, the official stops the stopwatch.

I could just see myself springing out of the plane, sliding down the smooth bottom of the canoe while it was still tied to the float, and landing in the water between the plane and the dock. No thanks.

Another event was the takeoff and landing competition. Two planes line up, idling, side by side, waiting for the starter to drop the red flag. Once the signal is given, both pilots give their planes full power and race to see who can get off the water first.

One of the rules is that they have to stay in the air, meaning they cannot stall or run out of fuel. Staying in the air is carefully noted, since the pilots remove all possible weight from their planes, including any extra fuel. Seats, other than the pilot's, rugs, tools, etc., are left in a pile on shore. I had no intention of flying a plane that close to running out of fuel. Too scary for my taste.

But there was another event called the Poker Run that sounded adventurous enough for me.

In 2010, Jenny and I decided to compete. Jenny lived in Bath, on the coast, with her husband, John, and I lived in the Lakes Region, miles away with Jim. We seldom saw each other during the year, so we made it a point to spend time together during the Fly-In.

We volunteered our time on the eight-to-ten-a.m. shift at the Katahdin Wings table, informing the public about the International Women Pilots Association called the Ninety-Nines. The 99s are a powerful support group for women interested in flying. We did our best to encourage women to fly, mentioning the many scholarships the organization offers to women to help them pay for flight training.

We had the rest of the day to shop at Beth's, our favorite homemade sweater vendor, and to watch some of the events prior to flying the Poker Run. This was a 175-nautical-mile route around northern Maine to four sporting camps to pick up the cards. Jenny would select a card at one stop and then I would at the next, and we took turns flying each leg.

As a flight instructor, I've spent hundreds of hours sitting in the backseat in a tandem airplane while instructing pilots. Jenny was a good seaplane pilot. We were both comfortable with her flying my plane. Sometimes it's fun for me to just sit and take in all the sights instead of being the pilot. As an instructor, I'm always the pilot in command as I sit in the backseat, but with an experienced pilot in the front, it was fun for me to relax.

When we signed up at the registration booth, we were given a sheet of paper with a list of the stops. Beside each location was the latitude and longitude of each camp. Then to the right was a small box to put in the number and suit of the card and another box for the initials of the representative affirming we had legitimately selected that card. We were to choose a card at each stop to complete the five-card hand. We selected our fifth and last card at a seaplane base in Millinocket, where we also fueled the plane.

Each stop used a deck of cards, so it wasn't one deck divided, which would be the normal way to play poker. Probably not the best way to set up a poker run, but we didn't care.

We flew almost the same route for 14 years and never had a good hand until 2019 when we won with a pair of 8s. Before that, we had an occasional pair of 2s, but that never created any excitement for us.

Approximately eight to ten planes participated in the Poker Run every year, and I looked forward to it more than anything else during the Fly-In weekend.

The route was designed to be flown counterclockwise, but we flew it in the opposite direction. It didn't really matter which way we flew. If we couldn't reach a stop, the cards could be selected back in Greenville. The real purpose was to see and experience flying in the great northern woods of Maine. The area was so expansive that traffic was not an issue going counter to the planned route.

There was no time limit. It could be flown either Friday or Saturday, depending on the weather. We wanted to land on Moosehead Lake at The Birches in the morning to take advantage of the calmer morning winds. Moosehead can be treacherous for a seaplane in the afternoon, with very rough conditions. We all know how to land in rough water, but handling a seaplane on the water is very difficult in strong winds. There was usually another plane at the dock at The Birches, so I never wanted to take a chance of damaging another plane or mine.

Our choice was to fly north to The Birches on the west shore of Moosehead Lake, then on to Penobscot Lake in western Maine on the Canadian border, Chesuncook Lake House in the central northern part of the State, Bradford Camps on Munsungan Lake, further east and on the north side of Mount Katahdin, then circumventing east of Katahdin to the Millinocket seaplane base. After picking up our last card and fueling there, we would head back to Greenville. There wasn't a better way to spend the day, as far as I was concerned.

The flight from Greenville to Rockwood was over the water, so I flew 500' above it and enjoyed the sparsely settled shoreline, along with a variety of islands barren of any indication of life. I imagined how peacefully some animals lived there, protected from outsiders.

After landing and picking up our card, we met some other pilots at The Birches who were lingering over cups of coffee in the pine-paneled dining room as they enjoyed the warmth of a roaring fire in the enormous fieldstone fireplace. Of course, we had to chat before we could go to our next stop.

This flight took us over land that was hilly and green with mountains off in the distance. The first year we flew there, we couldn't find the camp. Unfortunately, Penobscot Lake was misnamed on the aviation chart. We hunted around the area and on a lake just north of where we were directed, and we found a place that looked like it had the possibility of being a sport-ing camp. We were right. They were waiting for us.

After landing safely at the Penobscot cabins, Francine, a French-Canadian cook, served us wonderful warm, chewy chocolate chip cookies that were perfect with a cup of hot cocoa. Cookies are fine any time of day.

We sat at a well-worn round table in the sunny old-fashioned kitchen. Of course, we couldn't eat and run, so we sat there and got caught up on how business had been for the year. I was sitting there looking at history as Francine spoke in her lovely French accent. She was the former cook at the Chesuncook Lake House. Since that visit, I've thought of so many questions, but unfortunately didn't think of any to ask at that time.

Next, we were off to the Chesuncook Lake House, which has since tragically burned to the ground, on the west end of Chesuncook Lake. The first time we competed, it was a challenge to find this spot because the lake is 22 miles long. The latitude and longitude given simply brought us to the lake, not to the Lake House.

There were only 12 year-round residents in town, so you can imagine it was not a metropolis to find. We landed and pulled the plane up to the beach, secured it out of the wind, and walked about a half mile to the Lake House.

At this historic spot, they raised their own buffalo, so buffalo burgers were the main attraction. Jenny is not a strict vegetarian, but buffalo meat was out of the question for her. She opted for tuna instead. Both of our sandwiches were served on homemade bread. The side of fresh-cut fries were the best of the weekend.

I loved the atmosphere there. The loggers had marked their history with their cleated boots, creating pock-marked floors. Those marks were also on the stairs leading up to the spacious bathroom that had an old claw-footed tub. The huge window at the end of that room had thin white curtains that waved into the room on a gentle breeze as the sun brightened the room. The loggers had found comfortable lodging at that inn after working in the woods during harsh winter days.

The first few years in Chesuncook, we walked through the woods an additional half mile to "The Store." This was a one-man operation on the screened front porch of his home, where he sold homemade fudge and ice cream. It was never too early or late in the day for either of us to enjoy an ice cream cone. We used to sit in the front yard at a weathered picnic table beside a split-rail fence covered with fragrant red, white, and yellow roses. I clearly remember sitting in the warm sun one September afternoon having to quickly eat my ice cream to keep it from melting down my arm.

Leaving Chesuncook and heading east, we approached Mount Katahdin from the west and continued around to the north, landing close to the Bradford Camps on Munsungan Lake. These sporting camps were nestled down between the mountains, creating a welcoming site. We started having lunch there after the Chesuncook Lake House burned.

After selecting our card, we enjoyed Karen and Igor Sikorsky's hospitality. Igor, the grandson of the inventor of the Sikorsky helicopter, always had a project to work on, whether it was repairing a porch on one of their log cabins or tending the storage in the icehouse. He was patient with all the pilots coming in asking him questions, even though he was busy.

I asked Karen how they kept their perishable products cold without electricity. I knew they wouldn't run a generator all day to do that. She was nice enough to take the time and show us the small gray-shingled building close to the kitchen and not far from her huge vegetable garden. The building was half full of ice blocks separated by sawdust.

When we had that tour, it was September and the ice had been harvested the previous winter. When asked how that was done, Karen said, "Igor and a group of friends came up during the winter and stayed for a week cutting and hauling ice. This in an annual outing for these men, and they all look forward to it each year."

As I stood there listening, I imagined the phone calls planning which week they would come, and who had access to a snow machine with a utility trailer. I wanted to be there to see the operation. I thought about arriving by car hauling their snowmobile trailers. I didn't know how long it took them, but if I left from home in Naples, it would have taken me six hours to drive in good conditions. They lived further south. The last part of their trip, they would have to use their snow machines over the unplowed access road leading to camp. I imagined them getting there in the dark, starting fires in the woodstoves first, and then gathering all their supplies for the week ahead.

After a big breakfast the next morning, I imagined they went onto the ice and started cutting. Their blocks were 12" x 12" x 36", weighing over 100 pounds each. I got chills thinking about the wind whipping down the lake and burning any uncovered skin on their faces. Those blocks were then dragged over the ice and snow into the icehouse and covered with sawdust.

I'm sure there was great care given to safety, for if anyone fell into the water, they could quickly succumb to hypothermia. I didn't want to ask about that, but assumed ladders were out on the ice just in case. If they fell in the water, having something to hold onto while others dragged them out would have been much safer than anyone leaning over and potentially falling in.

I decided I would have been in the way, so I never asked if I could help. I know for sure I didn't want to do all the cooking for them. I wanted to be outside with them.

Jenny and I carried on conversations with the pilots, asking them where they had lunch, how their selected cards were, and what planes they were flying.

On our way to Millinocket Lake, I always marveled at the majestic formation of Katahdin, towering to sharp narrow ridges with deep valleys along the side. I couldn't imagine hiking along that ridge as I, like many pilots, have a fear of heights. It would be a terrifying experience for me to attempt that. I had no reference to the ground while in a plane, or anything holding me there, so I have never experienced that feeling while flying. I also feel in control when flying a plane, but I wouldn't walking along a ridge where I could easily trip or roll an ankle and plummet down hundreds of feet, bumping and banging into boulders along the way.

Katahdin is either the start or the end of the Appalachian Trail. If traveling from south to north, as most people do, the last 100 miles is called the Wilderness Trail, with no services along those treacherous miles. I could only imagine the variety of emotions people feel while hiking a steep, rugged trail and reaching the top of a 5,268' mountain, ending an arduous 2,184-mile hike that took months to accomplish.

We circled over the Millinocket seaplane base, crossed over the wires that ran along the Golden Road next to the base, landed smoothly in the cove, and taxied back to the dock. Jim Strang was the charter pilot who maintained the base. He would fly passengers to their island retreat or a rental cabin, where they stayed to fish for the week.

He always stood by at the dock in case anyone needed help. Operating the seaplane base in Naples for four years, and then teaching seaplane pilots even longer, gave me the experience I needed to reach the dock without any trouble or need for assistance. However, seaplane pilots are always ready to help.

Fueling the plane while it is on the water is a balancing act and nothing like fueling it on land at an airport. I would hold the fuel hose over my shoulder, step up onto the step above the float just in front of the wing, and turn around. I found it easier to balance while I leaned against the plane in order to reach the fuel cap on top of the wing. One 30-gallon fuel tank was in each wing. I only needed 15 gallons on each side to replace the fuel I had burned since leaving home. And while years of experience helped me with that job, Jenny was always there to help, handing me the fuel hose after I got settled on the plane.

The total flying time for the day, including circling to land, taxiing into and back out for takeoff, took us two and a half hours. But we always enjoyed ourselves so much at the different locations, it took us all day.

Awards were given out at the Saturday night banquet. In 2019, when we received first place for our pair of 8s, I was thrilled to walk up to the front of the crowded hangar to pick up my blue ribbon and plaque for bragging rights. Jenny had headed home earlier that day, so the person sitting beside me, using my phone, took a picture so I could send it to her. After sitting down at the table to finish my dessert, a tall young woman approached me.

"Would it be all right if I spoke to you?" she asked.

"Of course it is," I said.

"I've been thinking about learning to fly and wasn't sure it was a good idea because I've only seen male pilots. But here you are, not only flying but right in there competing with them," she said.

It never occurred to me that I was competing with men, but it impressed her. I was happy that I didn't say, "Yes, but it was only a poker run."

"You've inspired me so much that I will start lessons when I get home," she said.

I was astonished and pleased that a simple act of enjoying myself had encouraged another woman to fly. I never would have expected that would affect someone like that, but it made my day. She gave me a big hug as she left.

Jenny and I had started the weekend working at the Katahdin Wings booth telling women about flying. This young woman demonstrated to me that showing was better than telling.

The Birches dining room

Chesuncook Lake House and Cabins

Bradford Camps

Katahdin Air

Our typical route flying the poker run

Cutting ice blocks

End of day of ice cutting

Hauling into ice shed for summer storage

THE BOMB DROP

One year at the International Seaplane Fly-In, Mark Gilbert convinced me to enter the Bomb Drop competition. Mark was a friend who, along with his dad, ran the Moosehead Marina in the town of Rockwood. He wanted to fly in the worst way, but never had the time to take the required training. With his encouragement as the bombardier, I only had to fly the plane. I could do that.

I was flying my favorite plane that year: N3635M. It was a white PA-12 Super Cruiser with small green lines as detail. For this competition, the important part of this plane was the ability to open the top part of the door in order to unload our armament: grapefruits.

One at a time we were to aim for the middle of the markers on the lake. The team that got the closest won bragging rights for that year. We had two opportunities to accomplish this, but by the time the grapefruit hit the water, we were long gone and didn't have a clue if we were accurate or not.

I don't remember anything that stands out from that first Bomb Drop except that we had fun flying together.

The following year, I would fly and Mark would be the bombardier again. However, my favorite plane was not available, so I flew one of my seaplane school planes. It was the same model with tandem seating. That meant Mark would be in the front seat because there was no window to open in the back of the plane, nor could we open the top part of the door. The door itself would have to be open, and I didn't want to fly that way.

Mark, in the front without a pilot's license, wasn't an issue. I was a flight instructor, and sitting in the back of a tandem-seat plane was not out of the ordinary. I had dual controls back there and taught from that position all the time.

The two large orange buoys floating on the water at the seaplane base were separated by about 30 feet. I flew as slow as I could and maintained

200 feet above the water as directed, and Mark had centrifugal force to think about. Sounds easy, right?

Mark had to consider those issues, and I flew left or right, following his directions.

The bottom line was, we had an incredible amount of fun doing this as a team.

On our second and last chance to hit our target, I could see black clouds coming in from the west and close to the seaplane base. After we dropped our bomb, I decided to go directly to camp, where I could secure the plane at the dock.

When we landed in the cove at camp, expletives flew out of my mouth with no control. "Shit, shit, shit...!" A year's worth, as I remember. That word slips out of my mouth on occasion when I least expect it, but that day it kept flowing with no sign of stopping.

"What's wrong?" said Mark. "What did I do?"

"We just paraded ourselves around hundreds of seaplane pilots in Greenville with our water rudders down!"

"I am so sorry," he said.

"No, this is my fault, Mark. I'm the instructor."

I was furious at myself. This is the mortal sin of flying a seaplane. When caught doing so, one has to buy dinner for everyone! It's not something you ever escape. Pilots are always ready to take the attention off of their own mistakes, but the kidding is always done in fun.

I never bought any dinners. Sometimes there are benefits to being a woman with gray hair, but I have looked back many times and wished I could have at least bought everyone a drink that night!

The following year, we planned to enter the same competition, and I flew that same plane to our camp in Rockwood on Wednesday to be ready. (*Camp* is a common name in Maine for a vacation home.)

There was something that didn't sound right on Saturday morning when I started the plane, so I returned to the dock and left it there. I texted Mark and explained the circumstances. He seemed to understand.

I met Mark's wife, Deidra, later that morning at the seaplane base, and she gave me a different description of Mark's response.

"Mary, Mark was so upset, he disappeared out the door grumbling profanities and didn't come back for half an hour."

"I am so sorry. I had no idea this meant so much to him."

She said, "He looks forward to flying with you in this event all year."

While the Bomb Drop was going on without us, I went over to chat with Gordon Richardson, a friend and Super Cub pilot who was sitting on his floats waiting his turn. Gordon's plane was on amphibious floats, so he was able to keep it out of the water in front of the exposition hangar.

"Where's your plane this year, Mary?"

"It didn't sound right this morning, Gordon, so it's back at camp. We won't be competing this year."

"You can fly my plane."

A normal response from me would have been, "Oh, no thank you, Gordon," but that's not what I said.

"Thank you very much. I really appreciate that."

I ran over to Mark and told him to get the official entrant's bright Kelly-green T-shirts, gaudy that year with big letters across the top of the back that said CONTESTANT. "You do that, and I'll go register and get the two grapefruits."

My job only took me five minutes, and when I turned around, the plane, positioned on top of the ramp ready to go into the water, had Mark sitting in the backseat with a smile that went from ear to ear. I climbed onto the floats and into that front seat like I belonged.

This plane was configured with a window on top of the door that could be opened, so Mark didn't need to fly from the front seat. Immediately, we were signaled to get started. No time to put on our lovely green shirts; the air traffic controller was waiting for us.

I put my seat belt on and started the plane with my feet firmly planted on the brakes to prevent us from rolling down the ramp into the water. Needing to have permission to go down the ramp, I expected to sit there a moment or two. But as soon as the plane started, down we went. The brakes refused to hold.

"Oh brother! Ready or not, here we go," I said.

This didn't bother Mark at all. He was all in for the adventure.

"Do you know what the frequency is this year for the seaplane base?" I asked.

"No. How would I know?"

That made sense, but I was grasping for straws.

When we got into the water, I needed to bring the gear up and put the water rudders down to control the plane in the water.

"Good Lord," I said. "Where is the lever for the water rudders?" Mark was giggling in the backseat. "Oh, I found them."

Thoughts swirled around in my head: Where is the control for the gear? I can't take off with the wheels down.

I have thousands of hours flying seaplanes, but every plane is different, and I had never flown this one before. I had been with Gordon as an instructor while I sat in the backseat, but I'd never handled the water rudders or the gear, which were only accessible from the front. Once I got that all figured out, I heard a conversation with two other pilots and got the correct frequency for the seaplane base. We were ready.

I followed Mark's directions as I had last year, "Fly a little left...a little right."

The two flights were flown without incident and we landed.

You never know if you've won until the banquet the following night. We had fun and thought that was all that mattered. There was no parading around town with water rudders down that year, so I was happy about that.

When we finished dinner the following night and listened to the awards being given out, our name was called as the winners of the Bomb Drop competition. We decided that it was important for both of us to receive that award, so we went to the front of the room together to accept the plaque for our bragging rights of the year. Mark kept the second-place one from the year before, insisting that I was the one to keep the first-place trophy.

I treasure that award. It's hanging in my "She Shed," my hangar at the Auburn/Lewiston Airport.

I'm thrilled that I took the risk, entered those competitions, and accepted the fact that I'm not perfect.

I will never forget those flying experiences and how much fun they were.

Mary and Mark sitting at the top of the ramp in Gordon's plane in 2017

TRIALS AND TRIBULATIONS

In 2008, 16 years after I earned my pilot's certificate, my dream appeared to fully come to fruition with the purchase of a seven-seat Quest Kodiak I found in Texas. Little did I know that the dream would quickly turn into a nightmare.

I had started my charter seaplane business with a Cessna 180 on amphibious floats. It was a great start, but the plane was limited to only three passengers.

I would pick up one man in Boston on Friday afternoons and fly him to his second home in Vermont. Another customer had a second home on Thompson Lake in Maine. I regularly flew him from there to the Beverly airport in Massachusetts. However, they both wanted to have their families along on the flights. Flying for an hour over the mountains into a crystal-clear pristine lake sure beat a four-hour drive in traffic on a Friday afternoon.

One passenger frequently asked if I had ever considered a larger plane, and I explained that what a bigger plane would cost—$2 million to $3 million—was beyond me.

He asked if I had considered a loan.

I hadn't even thought about it because I couldn't afford the insurance deductible if anything ever happened. He then explained that he would be willing to support a larger plane. We started looking for a suitable aircraft to fit his needs.

I thought, This can't be really happening to me. I've wanted to do this for over thirty years and had given up on it. I certainly didn't expect this to happen. I've never heard of such a thing.

My good fortune in the seaplane industry was continuing.

I contacted the Cessna Caravan distributor and arranged for a plane to meet us at the Hanscom Airport in Bedford, Massachusetts. Marvin was the interested investor. He and his wife met me there, and we discussed all the wonderful places they could go as a family in that plane on amphibious floats. When looking into the specifications of the Caravan, I found it was not suitable for short-field operations, and I wanted to be able to bring the plane in and out of our field for storage after the seaplane season was over. The grass strip at the seaplane base was only 1,000 feet long, and the Caravan needed much more room.

My husband, Jim, had seen the Quest Kodiak in Alaska and thought that it would fit the bill nicely. He'd seen it take off in a very short distance from a grass strip and was quite impressed.

I discovered that Wipaire was installing a new float designed specifically for that plane, and the National Fish and Wildlife Foundation had purchased nine sets of floats for their Kodiaks. I looked at the specifications and found they almost matched the Caravan on floats as far as speed and fuel burn, so all my calculations were based on that information. The biggest advantage was that it was a STOL (short field takeoff and landing) plane.

I worked on how much it was going to cost to fly the plane per hour, and my bookkeeper worked on putting together an offer for Marvin. He wanted to confirm 60 hours of flight time a year, and I was to use this plane for other customers, too. He didn't want to be connected to it in any way other than financing. We had to be sure the pilots, maintenance, fuel, and general upkeep of avionics costs were all going to be covered, not to mention the expense of insurance. There were hidden costs that kept coming up, so many hours were spent trying to set the hourly fee accurately.

I finally found a beautiful Kodiak in Texas that was for sale and arranged for it to be delivered to Wipaire in Minnesota. I started a new corporation for the intended charter flights and waited anxiously for the plane to arrive in Maine so I could get started.

I had a careful pre-buy inspection done prior to the purchase and trusted Wipaire to have designed an appropriate set of floats for the Kodiak and for them to do the installation. Wipaire had been in the business of designing floats for over 40 years, and I had flown a much smaller amphibious float on my plane for several years.

I had visited Wipaire's plant on two different occasions, and I felt my decision was sound. My normal way to purchase anything new was to wait and see how successful it was in the market. I don't believe I have ever been the first in line to buy. That decision to purchase a new combination of plane and float so soon was a first for me.

Kodiak on wheels

There wasn't a float from any other company to fit the plane at the time. The Caravan always looked "under floated," meaning the floats needed to be bigger to keep them further out of the water. I've seen the aft end of the floats under water as the Caravan sat in the water at a seaplane fly-in, and it wasn't impressive. The larger float developed for the Kodiak would help the plane take off faster due to less drag in the water.

The manufacturer of the Quest Kodiak also made floats, but their design wasn't finished and therefore not ready by the time Wipaire had their floats ready to be installed. I'm sure that was why the rush was put on by Wipaire to be the first and only float available for that configuration on the market. Timing was everything.

I asked our friend Joe Dole to come to Minnesota to train in the Kodiak with me. As a retired airline pilot, he had more experience flying larger planes. I had more seaplane time than he did, so I was convinced the combination would be great. He and I would fly customers together until we were both proficient.

We worked very hard in our ten hours of training in Minnesota in that 7,000-pound aircraft on amphibious floats. When one person was flying, the other sat in one of the rear seats to observe.

Joe was very strong and had no trouble bringing up the water rudders prior to takeoff. They were only supposed to be in the water when doing slow taxi and had to be retracted during flight. If left down, they would get damaged during high-speed taxis and when landing. Due to the carbon fiber construction of those rudders, they didn't stay in the water when they were down. Therefore, heavy-duty springs were installed to hold them down, but made them very difficult to lift out. That was done with a lever on the floor. Its placement was slightly behind and to the right of the pilot's seat, making it very difficult for me to reach and haul up and forward. I was convinced by our instructor that others were able to do it, so I made sure I did. Not being able to take rudders out of the water was not going to stop me from flying that plane.

I never felt ten hours was enough training, but that's what everyone got, so I thought I would eventually get caught up with Joe's help. I could do what I was expected to do, but never felt comfortable and ready to fly on my own.

We flew from South St. Paul airport in Minnesota and landed at the Hanscom Airport to show Marvin. Joe wanted me to fly that leg to show the plane and he was right, but I was tired. I made a short turning approach to the runway just like I do on floats, and for the first time ever, the air traffic controller said, "Nice approach and landing." Marvin was listening on the radio and heard it, too. We were off to a good start.

Then I flew home to the Brandy Pond Seaplane Base in Naples, Maine, to receive a warm welcome from friends and family.

The following Sunday, Joe and I were practicing for our FAA check-ride that was coming up on Tuesday. In order to fly passengers for compensation, we had strict FAA guidelines to follow. The first step was a check-ride from my Principal Operations Inspector (POI), who would be coming out from the FAA Flight Standards District Office in Portland, Maine.

The day was very hot. Normally, Joe flew the first leg when we practiced, but that day I decided to fly first because I needed to experi-

Kodiak on floats at Brandy Pond Seaplane Base

ence a cold start and going down the ramp into the water. I had come up out of the water several times, so I needed to experience going down into it. Cold starts in an airplane can be very different from hot starts, so I wanted that experience. Joe also needed to experience coming up the ramp and how to counteract the airplane's left-turning tendency.

I felt wonderful flying that day. I pretended the visibility was poor, so I flew an instrument approach into the Fryeburg airport. Everyone flying in the area was congratulating me over the radio on my new purchase. Those pilots knew what an accomplishment it was for me to own and fly that plane. Pilots normally use only necessary aviation announcements at non-towered airports, so the conversations were a surprise and fun for me. Everything went well and I felt wonderful. I came out of the "clouds," banked right, and landed on Lovewell Pond.

I was thrilled my flying was going so well, and I felt like I belonged in that pilot seat that day. I can do this, I thought.

I took off from Lovell Pond, left the clear blue water and flew over to the Auburn/Lewiston airport for lunch. It was just a great morning.

After lunch, when it was Joe's turn, the wind had picked up from the southwest and we were sweating profusely in the plane, even though he got it started right away. Opening the window on the pilot's side let in fumes from the engine, so we were cooking.

Joe took off and was comfortable flying instrument approaches into the Auburn/Lewiston airport. What we both needed was more practice using the Garmin G1000 all-glass panel. We were both accustomed to steam gauges that were much easier to understand. The glass panel had constantly moving airspeed and altitude figures and created distractions we could do without. He went on to practice some steep turns. He, too, felt good about handling that oversized bird.

When we first got in the plane after lunch he said, "Today, I don't want you to say anything unless there is an emergency of some sort."

"Okay." I used the lever under the front of my seat to slide my seat back and folded my arms to indicate a hands-off position. The seats were adjustable to accommodate long or short legs and getting in and out of the plane.

Had I been telling him what to do? No, I didn't think so. Had I messed around with the GPS and distracted him? Yes. He probably wanted to be able to do it all himself, and I certainly understood that. The only problem with my seat being back was that I couldn't reach the rudders to help out if needed. I had to be able to do that as an instructor, but that was not my role that day.

On Sunday afternoons in August, you could be sure there would be lots of boats on Brandy Pond. It was usually next to impossible on a Sunday to find a place to land clear of their treacherous wakes. If we hit one while landing, it would be just like running into a granite curb with your car while trying to park. Add 80 mph to that mixture and it could easily damage the float attachments on a seaplane.

We were landing in a slight crosswind, which was something we always practiced in a seaplane, but add the heavy boat traffic and wakes, and it made our landing more demanding. He circled to see if he could find a better spot, but the boat traffic didn't improve. Everyone was out to find a place where they could stay reasonably cool on that hot day.

He was heading toward a jumble of cross-wakes when I broke my silence suggesting he land a little further north where the water was smoother. He added power and touched down in the best available spot. Adding power just before landing is common when handling a seaplane, but we had never practiced that with our instructor. Not a big deal to either of us—neither of us saw it as a problem.

It was also quite normal to keep that power in to do a step taxi, or fast taxi in laymen's terms. It's actually in the Kodiak on Wipaire floats landing checklist that it can be done. I didn't expect him to turn, but again, not a big deal and certainly nothing to be concerned about. I didn't bring my seat forward and didn't say anything. I sat there with my arms folded. I thought everything was going just fine.

The left float lifted out of the water. As the plane tipped more and the right wing got closer to the water, I realized we were in trouble. It was too late. We were going to cartwheel!

I must have some sort of survival mechanism that always takes over in a dangerous situation, because I was calm. We're going over and I knew what to do: Stay calm and wait for the plane to settle. That was something I taught all the time. The plane cartwheeled very fast, but it played out in slow motion for me. During the cartwheel, the seat belts locked me in place, but my head shook around like a rag doll. When the insidious ride finally stopped, Joe and I were still planted firmly in our seats. The instrument panel was still in front of us, but instead of blue sky in the windscreen, there was water. I knew we were upside down, but it happened so quickly I was disoriented.

It was eerily quiet except for my heartbeat pounding in my ears and the slight moaning of the plane as it settled in the water. That was an unusual situation to be in, but I must have been in shock, because I was not concerned.

Thank God the plane is built like a tank, I thought. The windows were still intact.

Joe looked at me as he tried to get out and said, "I can't open the door." We were still moving slightly.

The pressure was greater outside than it was inside, keeping Joe from opening the door. Completely relaxed, just as if this was practice, I said, "That's okay, Joe. When the plane settles, you can open the little fly window, and that will release the pressure. Don't undo your seat belt until you're ready to get out. You'll get tossed around if you do."

After things calmed down and the plane stopped moving, he opened the window. The water poured in and I undid my seat belt because the plane was tilted to the right and I was on the low side that was filling quickly. When Joe saw me taking off my belt, he thought he should take his off, too, but he was still out of the water. He fell on me, pinning me in the corner.

I thought, Oh, he is going to dislocate my knee after we've managed to survive a plane crash! This is incredibly painful, and I hope my knee survives intact.

I held my breath and waited for the cabin to fill more so he would float. The plane tipped more, and he could not reach the door. Finally, the cabin filled enough so he could float and could reach the door. He swam out.

"Follow me," he said.

There was so much water in the cabin after he opened the door, and it happened so quickly, that I floated enough to reach the door and start out. The plane continued to fill with water and sink further toward the bottom of the lake.

The door closed and had me pinned. It was crushing my gut and ribcage like a vise.

"DOOR!" was all that I could say as the plane sank further down into the steely cold Maine water. The pressure pushed out what little air was left in me.

I felt Joe's hand on my arm as the pressure of the door was released on my middle, and out I came from the plane.

Swimming toward the floats was what I was supposed to do from all my training, but it still didn't feel right. I was further down in the water than I thought. Air. I needed air. Would I ever get to the surface?

Relieved to reach the surface and breathe, I couldn't believe how many boats were all around the plane. There was a man swimming toward the inverted plane.

"Is there anyone else in the plane?" he asked.

"No. Get out of the water before you get hurt. There are too many boats out here!"

I was scared to death that someone was going to get hurt.

One boater offered to get us out of the water. I couldn't pull myself up and over the side of his boat. The man was pulling both of my arms as

Overturned Kodiak

my shirt rode up. I thought that was humiliating enough, but Joe was also pushing me with his hands on my butt. Thank heavens, I was finally in the boat in one piece with not a scratch on me. Joe was stronger and able to get himself in.

The driver was on the phone with the rescue squad. He told us, "They want us to go to the Moose Pond Marina right here."

"No thanks. Would you please take us to the seaplane base right over there?"

"They want to go to the seaplane base," he said into the phone. Then he turned to us and said, "The sheriff wants you to go to the marina."

"No, the seaplane base is where we belong," I said. "I'll take responsibility for this, so please take us there. That's home, and that's where we need to be."

He drove his boat to our dock and dropped us off.

"Thank you very much for bringing us home," I said as I stepped onto the dock. He quickly left the scene. I guess he didn't want to answer any questions or be responsible for not following orders.

My thoughts were focused on my phone as I walked with my head down along the dock. I couldn't get it open to dry it out. My thoughts were racing. My Blackberry was my freedom to stay out of the office. I couldn't lose my emails and phone calls, and I couldn't have that information deleted. But

I couldn't get the damn thing open! I almost walked into someone who turned out to be an EMT. He very kindly took my phone from me, opened it, and handed it back. I told him I was going to put it on the stump to dry.

"Sit over here, please," he said kindly, pointing to the two yellow chairs in front of the office in the shade of an oak tree. "We need to see if you're injured."

"I'm fine," I said.

"I am, too," said Joe.

At first, this was a great place to sit and watch what was going on, as the accident had created quite a lot of commotion. Cars were coming in and filling the yard, and boats seemed to be fascinated by a plane upside down in the water. Everyone was milling around.

"Joe, are you all right? Your leg is bleeding."

"Yes, it's nothing. When I opened the door to get you out, I scraped my shin."

Susan and Mike, my stepdaughter and her husband, arrived, and Susan called Jim, who was up at camp. He insisted on flying himself home. Mike kept the press away. Thank goodness. I am so grateful Mike was there and thought to do that! Later I was told that he told the news people, "If you come down here on this private property, I will personally pick you up and remove you!" Mike is 6'2" and about 300 pounds. They left.

Mike called my daughter Lisa, and she arrived visibly and understandably upset. I tried to comfort her and convince her that we were fine. We did just what we trained for all the time. I imagine I was a little too blasé, but I hated seeing her so frightened.

My bookkeeper, Sydney, arrived and squatted down in front of me leaning in for a hug. I burst out crying. We had worked so hard for months together, dealing with contracts, multiple customers, and the purchasing process, that I felt terrible for her and I finally released my pent-up emotions. Thank God we survived.

When a plane cartwheels like that, there is frequently a fatality. We did everything we had been trained to do, and fortunately the plane didn't fill with water right away. We also had seat belts and shoulder harnesses that kept us from flying forward and hitting our heads. Without a shoulder harness, a pilot is thrown forward and knocked unconscious. Unfortunately, a death often occurs because people cannot get out of the plane fast enough. We had survived. We were extremely fortunate to not be more injured than a nasty-looking scrape on Joe's leg.

As I checked for bruises, my fingernails were turning blue from sitting in the shade. We were both soaking wet, and even though it was a hot day, we were cold. I had multiple bruises on my belly, across my shoulders from the seat belts, and all over my legs.

We were not allowed to leave. I didn't understand why at the time. I felt trapped for no reason.

"Can't I just go to the house to put my phone in some rice and change my clothes?"

I was still frantic about the phone. My house was a short walk down the driveway.

"Not just yet," said the sheriff.

The State Police arrived and took over the investigation. I thought an investigation was strange, but of course, that was the normal procedure when there was an accident like this. He had a conversation with the sheriff, and our local constable was not happy.

One by one, Joe and I were asked to get into the state cruiser to answer questions. We both had an opinion as to what had happened, but we really didn't have an answer as to the cause of the accident. I had never seen a seaplane respond like that before and hadn't anticipated anything was going to happen. The officer wanted us in a closed vehicle to see if either of us had been drinking and to make sure our stories were the same. I can't imagine drinking and then trying to fly, but I guess that's a possibility. Our stories were certainly not the same. We didn't discuss what we thought had happened. We were just happy to be alive.

I asked again, "Can I please go down to the house to change? It's right there, just across the brook."

"You can, but come right back," said the officer after he was finished asking questions.

Joe's wife, Janie, arrived crying as she gave Joe a huge hug. She was stunned because Joe had been flying since he was a kid and never had an accident. Janie didn't think to bring clothes. As soon as Mike called her, she simply got in the car and came right over. Joe was shivering in shock, and

Lisa, thankful to have something to do, offered to go to his house and get him some dry clothes. He explained where they were and off she went.

"Why now?" Janie asked. "What happened?"

We didn't have an answer.

Tim Bickford, an aviation friend, walked into the yard and offered to help. He said he was going by and saw the commotion. Peter Marucci arrived with his scuba gear to help with getting the plane out of the water. Pete lived up the lake and had his own seaplane base on the west side on Long Lake. How he found out so fast was puzzling, but I was very grateful he and Tim were there.

"Thank you both for coming. I really appreciate this very much. Please don't do anything with the plane until Jim gets here. He has handled so many overturned seaplanes and knows how to do it without damaging it any further. He will want to supervise this process. Do you guys mind?" I asked.

"No. Of course not. I realize how knowledgeable he is," said Pete.

After Jim landed and idled the plane to the dock, I was frozen in place. Joe told me to go down and meet him, but I was scared to death he was going to be mad and say, "That never would have happened if I was in that plane!" He seemed emotionless but relieved to find we are both okay. There was no warm, welcoming hug, just the normal one. He went out in a boat to see what he needed to do and returned shortly after, saying, "They don't need me. They know what to do."

I forgot that Matt, who at that time had worked for me for several years, knew exactly how to care for the overturned plane. He had been with Jim recovering another overturned plane in Lovell just two weeks prior to our accident. He was giving the guidance that was needed. The friends simply arrived and went to work helping him. Friends are to be treasured!

Lisa came back with Joe's dry clothes and later with a wonderful pot of homemade soup. With dry clothes on after being allowed to go home, we enjoyed the soup on the porch. There was not much conversation during this delicious and much appreciated meal.

Jim Allen, the marina owner next door, called the crane company on Sebago Lake. We watched it slowly work its way on a barge from the Songo River at the southern end of Brandy Pond, and by the end of the day, the plane was secured to the crane.

The plane arrived at the dock in pieces at about 11:00 that night. It had been a long day, as the accident had happened at 2:15 p.m. The propeller was askew, and the floats dangled off to one side, hanging like a loose tooth. The right wing was damaged, along with the tail, and the rudders were curled and totally beyond repair. When the crane lowered the plane down, a horrible sound of crunching metal came from the lower section of the fuselage where one of the float struts had gone right into the side. The plane was a mess, but I did not want it to be further damaged.

Kodiak at the dock

The next morning...

The stench of jet fuel was overwhelming. How was I going to take care of getting that off the water? General aviation fuel evaporates, but this was jet fuel and apparently doesn't. It was floating toward the boats at the marina and I knew they wouldn't like it one bit.

"Mary, you've got to do something about this fuel. It's getting all over the hull of the boats in the marina," said Jim Allen.

I walked back to the house to try and figure out what to do. I went back in an hour without a solution. The fuel was off the water. Baffled, I saw long white absorbent tubes sitting on the ground. They were left over from the job of soaking up the jet fuel. The saturated ones were securely sealed in oversized black plastic bags beside the hangar. I was told by someone that a hazmat company was coming to pick them up. I never did find out who accomplished that messy job.

"Who took care of the fuel?" I asked.

"I don't know," said Matt, "but the FAA will be here soon to investigate for the NTSB."

The National Transportation Safety Board would have been there if there was a fatality, but in this case, the FAA would do the investigation. In the Federal Regulations, the NTSB is to be notified, and the State Police had taken care of that.

The crane had lifted the plane out of the water and Matt McFadden and Pete Marucci, both mechanics, were in the process of removing the floats and putting it on wheels. It was much worse-looking out of the water. The end of the wing was hanging precariously and the floats had been removed. Nothing looked right to me.

Charter flying was over for me. But instead of feeling regret, I felt relieved!

That accident could have happened in the Northern Maine Wilderness where there was no communication, colder water, and no boats around. My customers and their families could have been on board, and perhaps there could have been a fatality. Just the thought of it was more than I could stand.

I got the message. No more charter flying. I'm not one who normally gives up, but trying to get this started had not been as smooth as everything else I had done in aviation, so I decided to stick with flight training. Sometimes things just don't work out the way you think they will.

Shortly after my accident, another pilot had exactly the same issue when landing in Lake Hood in Anchorage, Alaska. At that time, the accident/incident rate for that combination of plane and floats was 42%.

AN UNEXPECTED SETBACK

In January of 2016, on a Thursday afternoon, a technician inspected my heart during a biannual ultrasound to make sure my aortic murmur had remained the same and had not gotten any worse. I was 71 at the time. If my primary physician had not told me years ago about this leaky valve, I would never have known it existed.

As the ultrasound technician examined my heart, she asked, "Do you have a cardiologist?"

"No. I've never needed one," I answered with an assertive tone. I was not pleased that she thought I should have one. My immediate thought was, What does she know? That was easier than thinking she knew what she was saying.

Silence from the technician. Asking a question like that was very unusual for someone in her position, because previous technicians had always told me they were prohibited from discussing any of their observations. Of course, I liked to ask anyway.

"I see you had an ultrasound done two years ago," she stated. "What were the results of that test?"

"The doctor said there was no change and that I looked very healthy."

A slight sound of disapproval came from her.

That made me uncomfortable. I had an inclination there was something wrong, but decided she would have sent me right back to the doctor if it was serious. When she told me the results would be read on Monday, I decided to keep my plans and head north to our camp on Moosehead Lake on Friday since the weather was forecasted to be good for flying: high ceilings, good visibility, and very little wind.

After a pleasant weekend, I wanted to fly on Monday. It was a clear, crisp, cold day, and I really wanted to be outside, so I called the doctor's office to get some answers. Since the ultrasound exam, I had felt uncertain about the results and wanted to make sure it was safe for me to fly. I could not wait for someone to finally get around to calling me, so I called the doctor's office myself. I wanted to get on with my day. Staying inside on a day like that was not an option.

"I plan on flying today and wonder if you have the results from the ultrasound."

"Let me look," said the pleasant woman who answered the phone. "No, but I'll check with the doctor to be sure it is okay for you to fly."

She called back in 15 minutes with her voice full of optimism.

"The doctor said these results always come back with your heart murmur in the same condition as the previous years, so she feels confident it will be fine this time, too."

I did not have the same level of confidence because of the technician's obvious questionable attitude, but I certainly felt healthy with no indication of anything being wrong, so I decided to fly. Besides, her comment was the answer I wanted to hear.

I wondered what life would be like without being able to fly. Would I find another activity to love? Would I produce the book people asked me to write? I've watched other pilots dive into despair when they stop flying, and I didn't want to do that. I quickly put all that out of my mind. That was not today's issue.

I enjoyed a beautiful day of flying. Outfitted with wheel-skis, I did several takeoffs and landings on the snow-covered frozen lakes in and around Moosehead Lake. The wheels penetrated about two inches below the skis, allowing me to roll the plane out of the hangar, taxi to the runway, and take off. When I landed on the snow, the wheels did not create appreciable drag, and the skis kept me from sinking deeply into the snow.

The conditions were perfect that day, with a pure white blanketed bed making me feel like I landed perfectly. I wondered if I could make it feel as good as that when I returned to Jackman and landed on a hard-surfaced runway with patches of ice.

For non-pilots, it is often thought that flying is to satisfy our need for speed. That has nothing to do with my joy, unless I need to travel a long distance. Even then, if I'm not pressed for time, flying low and slow is my preference. I like to see what the roads look like as they twist and turn through the woods. I wonder why people choose living close together in some places, or why some prefer to hide in the hills. How long does it take them to shop for groceries, and how far do they have to travel? Those thoughts are in addition to admiring the surrounding beauty with clear visibility due to fresh clean air, especially during the winter.

After I enjoyed myself for an hour, I flew back to the airport on the Canadian border that was only 20 miles from Moosehead Lake. I tucked the plane into the hangar where it would be safe from the unpredictable harsh weather of northwestern Maine. My side of the hangar always had the worst weather because it was facing the northwest. Along with drifting snow, it had ice that wanted to stay for the winter.

I took off my headset and pulled my warm wool hat down over my ears. There was a cool breeze, and the temperature was only 15 degrees, so I needed to move quickly when I got out of the plane. I wore multiple layers of clothing that made it awkward getting out of the plane. I needed all those on to keep me warm when out of the plane. The plane had plenty of heat, but when flying on skis and dealing with cold weather, I had to prepare for surviving if stranded, for some reason, in Northern Maine.

Life does not get any better. Flying forces me to pay attention to just what is happening and what I am going to do next. It's a state where I do not think of anything else that is going on in my life, nor what has gone on in the past. I do not contemplate tomorrow...just the day and the moment.

I study the shape of the clouds drifting overhead, the pink effect of the sun in the morning on the tops of trees, and the warm soft colors in the afternoon changing the color of the mountains in the distance to soft green tones. Perhaps that's why I am always at peace when flying.

I also did not think of the ramifications of having something wrong with my heart.

Before I got out of the plane, I put ice creepers on my boots to keep from sliding on the ice. I had to take them off before I went in the hangar so I wouldn't slip on the smooth surface of the cement. My fingers, exposed for only a few minutes, were freezing, and I found it difficult to take the creepers off. I put the plane away and drove back to the Moosehead Lake house.

I read a novel for the rest of the afternoon. Relaxing there was easier than at home. Being so remote, it was always quiet and peaceful. I never seem to find the same level of peace when I constantly see something I need to do at home.

After dinner that night, the phone rang at 7:30.

"Hello?"

"Oh, I'm so happy to hear you've landed safely," said the physician assistant. "The doctor said to tell you that wherever you are in this country, do not fly home."

My stomach clenched, and I thought, I'm not sure what kind of flying they think I do, but I don't go very far in an airplane that goes 90 knots, on skis, and only has two seats. However, this must be serious if she is calling at this hour.

"The ultrasound that was normal in the past shows some irregularities this time. We need you to have an electrocardiogram and a cardiac catheterization. In addition to those tests, we want you to have an appointment with a surgeon."

"Oh..." I said slowly, quite surprised. "When would you like me to make these appointments?"

"We will make them for you, and they should be completed within the next two weeks."

Good grief, I thought. Just how serious is this?

"Thank you for calling," I said. I wasn't at all thankful for that news.

On Tuesday morning, I left for home in the spare car I used to get back and forth to the hangar. On the way home, I decided to get a cardiologist. I wanted a specialist in the field to monitor all the tests I was to take and make sure I really did need surgery.

As directed by the doctor, I could not fly. I have made the trip to Moosehead driving many times, but only because I needed to bring something in the car that would not fit in the plane or the weather dictated driving instead of flying. Told I could not fly was a completely different story. How could I have something going on inside my body that I didn't feel but that could be dangerous? This was frightening.

I never did like being told I couldn't do something, but I would have to comply this time. I had worked so hard getting where I was and had no plans to disobey the rules. I enjoyed the respect I had from the aviation community and the FAA. I loved the guidelines pilots have to follow. I always did like boundaries—knowing what I could and could not do. But I was not particularly fond of this limitation.

Driving home from Rockwood to Naples takes four hours as opposed to one and a half when flying. There was no contest that flying was much more fun with lots more to see from 5,500 feet. I loved flying in between the mountains to see if I could spot any wildlife. During the winter, moose were easily seen, as their brown bodies and massive racks stood out against the pure white snow. They were frequently on the snowmobile trails, but I could also see them if they were browsing around deciduous trees. Driving, I am lucky to see a fox or a deer.

I have always driven myself to doctors' appointments unless medication was involved. Then it was mandatory I have a ride home. For the first electrocardiogram, Lisa drove me to Mercy Hospital in Lewiston. I wasn't going to be medicated, but emotionally I needed her, and she must have sensed that. Lisa wanted to be my advocate, one who is not the patient and hears what is being said without the emotion of the potentially frightened patient, or, like me, in denial.

The young woman who was about to perform the exam said, "This dye is iodine and will be injected into your vein. We will then be able to see all the details of your heart."

"I am allergic to iodine."

"Oh dear. Just a minute," she said as she left the room.

A thin mustached man, who I assumed would be behind the camera watching the dye flow through my arteries, came abruptly into the freezing-cold room. I had only been in the room for five minutes, but I was cold and impatient. He appeared aggravated by my concern.

He said, "This is a different form of iodine and will not bother you."

Convinced he knew what he was talking about, I said okay. I wondered why they did not know about this allergy in the first place since it is in my records. I had to depend on their knowledge of the contents of the dye.

The dye was injected into my left arm as I was lying on a narrow bed. I was then rolled into the narrow cylinder containing the camera. I can't imagine why a camera would make so much noise, but it clanked along taking multiple images. When they had the shots they needed, I was rolled back out.

"If you give us fifteen minutes, we would like to inspect these pictures. You can have a seat in the waiting room."

Lisa and I sat down on the hard, maroon plastic chairs. In less than five minutes, Lisa said, "Mom, the whole side of your face is breaking out in hives."

I did not feel that anything different was going on, but she took me by the hand right back into the examining room.

"My mother is having a reaction to the iodine."

The young woman assistant said, "Okay. Have a seat and we will give you some Benadryl."

She brought out a syringe and injected the antihistamine into a vein in my right arm. As the fluid started to flow from the needle, I grabbed the arms of the chair and said, "I feel faint."

With the Benadryl now in my system, and assisted into a wheelchair, Lisa was told to take me to the emergency room and instructed to stop by admissions so I could sign the mandatory paperwork. I could think clearly, but I could not talk. My mouth would not open. Asked to sign my name when we got there, I could not.

The gray-haired woman behind the desk responded to my blank stare by saying, "Your initials will be fine."

Expected to initial the documents, it was all I could do to raise my arm and make illegible scribbles near the line where I was expected to sign. I wondered if this was like having a stroke.

"This is ridiculous," said Lisa, as she wheeled me away in disgust. "We will have to do something about this so I can sign for you," she said.

Her comment was an unsettling indication of my losing control, and I was not in a hurry to do that. However, in this case, I thought maybe she *should* be able to sign for me since I was clearly NOT in control. I was not happy. I hated losing control.

Finally covered with some warm blankets in the emergency room, I relaxed. After 45 minutes, released from the hospital with my ability to speak restored, Lisa drove me home.

"Thank you for being there for me, Lisa. It was comforting knowing you would take care of my needs."

When I called the Maine Medical Cardiology department for an appointment, I was scheduled the following week with Dr. Sanjeev Francis.

It warmed my heart to have Lisa come with me again to this appointment. It was important to have a good advocate in this situation, and she was quick to offer her assistance in that capacity. I was not accustomed to being watched over, but delighted to have her by my side.

On the scheduled day, when the doctor came into the examining room, I knew our doctor–patient relationship was going to be perfect. He was a tall, dark skinned, perhaps Indian, and handsome man. He overflowed with kindness and confidence, and his face had a wonderful sincere smile.

After all the introductions and exam, he asked, "What symptoms have you had to alert you that you had an issue with your heart?"

"I have not had any indication or symptom."

"Have you experienced shortness of breath?"

"No."

"How about any signs of weakness?"

"No."

"Have there been any symptoms of being lightheaded?"

"No," ...again.

"Well," he said, "we usually like to see some symptoms prior to rushing into any kind of heart surgery."

"Well," I said. "Let's look at this a different way. Would you want me to go in for surgery while I'm healthy in all the other parts of my body, or should we wait for me to fall, hit my head, or have a car accident and then be admitted in an emergency?"

He smiled and said, "I think you have a point. Let's see what the surgeon has to say."

Unfortunately, the first electrocardiogram was at Mercy Hospital and the results were not transferred by the same computer system to Maine Medical. I had to go through all that again. Dr. Francis assured me I would not have the same reaction.

"They will medicate you first with Benadryl and it will be in your system prior to the dye being injected. This test is very important for us to see the condition of the valve prior to surgery."

I did have another electrocardiogram, and yes, I did have a reaction, but it wasn't as severe.

On the way home from that first appointment, I began to think more about what symptoms I may have had that Dr. Francis was looking for. Then it came to me: I'd had an episode one hot day that must have been related to my faulty valve. I walked to the post office that was only a mile away and could not make it home. Frightened, I wasn't sure I would make it to a chair or someplace to sit down before fainting. I stopped about halfway down the hill at the seaplane base on Long Lake and pretended to be fine. I chatted with Matt, the seaplane pilot and former employee, hoping the cool breeze off the water would help to stop the perspiration from covering my face. I waited for the lightheadedness to go away, but it did not. After half an hour, I called my son-in-law Ed and asked if he would pick me up. He and Anna were staying in the guest house for a few months while they were trying to locate a suitable house for sale in North Carolina where they wanted to live. I thought Anna was busy on a proposal and didn't want to bother her.

Ed brought me the short distance home and I sat on the porch for another half hour drinking ice water. I blamed myself for this experience. I hadn't eaten any protein or drunk any water before I left for the post office. I called my primary care physician's office concerned, because the lightheadedness didn't go away.

One of the nurses called me back.

She said, "Mary, I just spoke to the doctor, and she said if you still feel this way in an hour, call us back."

Continuing to blame myself, the dizziness eventually went away. This was more than likely the "lightheadedness" Dr. Francis was asking about. What else had I experienced during the previous months? I couldn't remember anything in particular.

My two daughters, Anna and Lisa, came with Jim and me to the appointment with the surgeon to hear his opinion on the next step. Anna flew into Portland from some distant city the night before. I never knew where she was in the United States. She was sought after as a restaurant consultant, and I could not keep track of her. I was comforted by her willingness to interrupt her busy schedule to be with me at that time.

We all met at the doctor's office two blocks down the steep hill from Maine Medical Center where I was to have surgery...if necessary. I was still hopeful there had been some elaborate mistake and I would not need to have an operation. I was alone during the exam, and then we all sat in a cramped private waiting room with just enough chairs for us and waited for the doctor. This particular room was too similar to a private room in a funeral home, and it made me uncomfortable.

Having the little artificial heart valve in a glass case did little to comfort me, but I did not share this gory information with my family. I was still being the mother and trying to protect them from any fears of my own.

The PA came in first and informed us of the details of how the day of the surgery would proceed. Among the scary thoughts about having open-heart surgery, he included the fact that this event could be fatal. To me, this was a given fact. I have had many operations, and prior to each one, was told they could possibly end in a fatality. I assumed there was much more of a risk of not waking up this time than with any other operation. I was not sure what was going through the thoughts of my family, but I assumed I was the one that was more comfortable in this situation. I either would wake up or not.

One of the gifts my mother gave me when I had my appendix removed when I was five was a good description of what I would experience in the hospital, along with a very positive attitude toward successful results: I would receive breakfast in bed and medicine to alleviate the pain. This attitude has helped me to pass right through fear and look forward to getting better. Thank you, Mom.

The PA went on to say I would be on an inhalator and recovery would be in the Cardiac Intensive Care Unit until I was stable. This was all matter-of-fact, as if we heard this information every day. I have always felt that being the patient is much easier than it is for the spouse or for the children. My girls were 45 and 50 at the time, but I was still their mother.

The doctor came in and explained that I had a severely calcified aortic valve, and it was necessary that it be replaced. I wanted it fixed right away so I could go back to flying. I would do what I had to do to recover. To me, it was as simple as that.

How had I not known something as serious as this was going on inside my body? I never had any indication there was anything wrong. At least I didn't associate some symptoms with my heart. There was no history of heart issues in my family and, in the past, all medical exams had gone well.

I decided to take our families out for dinner at an upscale Italian restaurant to show my appreciation for their concern. It was wonderful to have some element of control by inviting the whole family, but, at the same time, I wasn't sure why I was doing it. I actually felt a slight amount of guilt. I was exerting my control while I might have frightened them with a gesture of "goodbye." I knew I was going to live through this operation and feel better afterward. My daughters and husband were more pessimistic than I.

The day of the operation, I received medication as I was waiting my turn. That was helpful, but I was alone, enclosed with sliding curtains surrounding my cubicle. If someone had been with me, I do not know what I would have wanted him or her to do or say. I did not want to feel so isolated in that little area waiting for my turn. That was all I remember as I drifted off to sleep while being rolled on my gurney into the operating room.

I did not want anyone to see me when I came out of anesthesia on a ventilator with a tube in my mouth and a machine pumping air into my lungs. I wanted to protect them from that image. I never gave it a thought prior to this experience, but during the surgery, a machine was circulating my blood while my heart was not beating. Another machine was breathing for me. Now it makes perfect sense, because how could a surgeon remove a valve and stitch in a replacement with my heart happily pumping away? I guess I did not want to think about it with all those details. Maybe I was not as relaxed as I thought.

During the discussion about my postoperative care, I was told my hands would be tied so I could not pull the tube out. That lack of control terrified me. Fortunately, my friend Jenny's sister-in-law had recently gone through open-heart surgery, and I asked to speak with her. I wanted to know what the experience was like for her. What was it like waking up in that condition, and not being able to do anything about using her hands?

"Mary, I was so heavily medicated, I knew it was there, but it didn't bother me," she told me.

This gave me a great deal of comfort. I thought at the time that was my only concern. I did not want to struggle and have someone tell me not to do something I wanted to do.

The Cardiac ICU was in a small well-lit room surrounded by machines of all shapes and sizes buzzing and beeping. I guess that was a good thing, because it meant I was alive. That was good. There was a wall of glass with a door keeping me isolated from the hall. My private male nurse was all mine, and he was thoughtful and efficient with his care. He simply said it was time to do something, and he did it. I do not remember everything, but I do recall how he smoothly removed a drain just under my diaphragm. He moved about the room preparing to do whatever else needed to be done.

I felt as if I were in a dream when coming out of anesthesia. I could sense people coming into the room. I felt a gentle comforting touch on my arm. The hand was warm. I couldn't see anyone. It was more like feeling their presence. The kiss on my cheek was soft and loving. Several kisses followed along with "I love you."

Do you know what it's like to have a dream that is so real you wake up startled because you have tried to move your arm, but you couldn't? That was what it was like for me. I didn't understand why I couldn't sit up and hug these wonderful, loving family members.

My mind wasn't at all clear, and I didn't realize my hands were tied. I can't imagine what it would have been like if they had not been secured to the side railing. There were tubes in my mouth, drains in my chest, electrodes attached everywhere to those beeping machines. There were also several stitches holding me together, along with IVs attached to my arm. It sounded to me as if those items needed to stay right where they were until someone else decided it was time for them to be removed. I was not capable of making any decisions.

The experience in the ICU of feeling that genuine love and affection, coupled with my inability to respond, led to tears slowly sliding out of the corner of my eyes as my family left the room. My capable nurse gently wiped those salty tears away with a soft tissue. He didn't need to say a word. I was overwhelmed with gratitude to feel so loved by my family.

That was not a frequent occurrence for me during that time of my life. In the years prior to that operation, I had tried to convince myself I was strong and didn't need to be reminded that I was loved. Respected for my work was not enough. I needed the loving care of warm arms around me. At least occasionally, I wanted to be held in the arms of my husband and kissed on the top of my head. I missed the smell of his clean manly skin and the comfort of his arms around me. I needed to hear the words of affection. They were missing.

Anna and Lisa worked out their schedules so at least one of them was in the hospital at all times. They told me they slept on the oversized brown leather recliners in the waiting room during the night. I loved having them come into my room several times to check on me. How fortunate I was to have such loving daughters who were so attentive and caring. I had love, thoughts, and prayers comforting me.

But I didn't have the breakfast in bed my mother had told me about. I had been throwing up and the thought of food was not inviting. I felt fortunate to have ice chips that Lisa fed me to moisten my mouth. Breakfast would come later when I was upstairs the following day...something light, of course, to make sure my system adjusted.

Sometime in the morning on the day after surgery, my nurse said, "Mary, you are doing so well you don't need to be down here any longer, but there isn't a room available for you upstairs just yet."

That was very good news to me. Not that they didn't have a room, but that I was doing well. Being the competitive person I have always been, I was sure I was way ahead of schedule and nestled back beneath my warm covers to rest so I could gain emotional and physical strength. I was grateful to be alive.

I was scared to get up, but I was not in pain. Would I stay stitched together? I was assured prior to surgery that pain would not be an issue because they would be cutting through bone. Not so sure I thought that was a good idea, to be using a saw on my chest, but I was comforted that I wouldn't have to deal with pain, and I didn't.

While recuperating in the hospital, I was visited each day by an attending physician. One day, one of those physicians used his cold stethoscope on my chest and my back, while I took the obligatory deep breaths in and out. He then said something I did not want to hear.

"It sounds like you have a little fluid in your lungs. I'd like to have an X-ray to see just what's going on."

I do remember being quite adamant about being just fine, because that's what I wanted to be...fine. But my opinion didn't seem to matter. Not long after that display of my professional opinion, I was whisked down the hall into the elevator and to the bowels of the hospital for an X-ray. About two hours later, another doctor whom I hadn't met before entered my room and informed me that there was fluid surrounding my lungs and that he would remove it.

"I will use a needle and go in through the ribs on your back," he said. "I'll be back shortly."

Good God. This sounds frightful to me, I thought. I was not accustomed to being scared, but I was that time.

I was shocked when he came back in with what looked to me like an 18" needle that included a huge syringe. Just the sight of it gave me thoughts of extreme pain. Fortunately, Lisa was there with me.

"You need to sit on the edge of the bed and lean over away from me," said the doctor in his extraordinarily efficient manner.

Lisa said, "Mom, I'll stay here with you."

I responded, "I'll be okay. Why don't you wait in the other room?" I really did not want to alarm her, or have her see me so vulnerable.

"I'm staying right here with you. Lean right against me and squeeze all you want," she said.

The physician said, "I want you to relax as best you can. This is going to hurt."

I was so scared to see the size of that needle attached to that huge syringe. I relaxed as best I could to make it easier for the doctor to insert the needle. It hurt more than I expected, but I squeezed Lisa, and screamed through gritted teeth as I buried my head in her shoulder. How did he know just where that fluid was? How did he know exactly where to insert the needle? Would he puncture anything else while the needle was in there? I wondered, but I felt safe with the efficient way he handled the procedure.

Lisa gave me more comfort than she could have imagined. I don't believe she had ever experienced me being frightened before. If she did, I'm not aware of it. She wasn't with me when I was flying to Alaska and the clouds came down and surrounded me when flying low between the mountains.

Lisa told me later that the syringe was filled with pink liquid when he took the needle out. So much for my intelligent opinion of not having any fluid next to my healthy lungs!

Day by day, I continued to feel better, and before I knew it, I was released to go home after being in the hospital for only five days. I had recovered well and came home two days sooner than we all expected. I could not allow myself to be vulnerable, so I planned on doing everything I was told.

When leaving, Lisa took some of the flower arrangements to other rooms that had none. I thought this was such a caring thought on her part, and I was proud to have a daughter think of others that way. My room had been filled with a beautiful display of color from caring friends.

Lisa and Anna continued to monitor my recovery, which pleased me more than can be imagined. Mothers simply never stop loving and adoring their children. I always have to remind myself that I need to let them go on with their own lives, but I would love to be more involved. I often wonder how to do that without being a pest.

I would not be able to fly for six months, so I busied myself in other ways to keep occupied. The day after my six months' limitation, I could then take the required tests to prove to the FAA that I was healthy enough to fly. An ultrasound and an electrocardiogram were performed, and I then wore a Holter monitor for 48 hours to register the rhythm of my heart.

The following week, I picked up all the test results, including the complete squiggly line report showing my heartbeat, and brought them to the FAA Medical Examiner in Dover, New Hampshire. His secretary packed all the information up and sent it to Oklahoma City for an official final check.

I was patient for twelve weeks, but furious when the person in the Oklahoma office contacted me.

"Some of the results from your Holter monitor are missing."

I held my tongue because I knew that everything was together when I'd brought the reports to Dover. It had taken them three months just to look at the paperwork. The missing material had apparently been lost somewhere between my doctor's office and Oklahoma City.

Rather than waste time fussing about this situation, I went to the hospital the following day to pick up the results of the tests again and sent them by overnight mail. In two weeks, I decided to follow up and make sure they had been received.

I was abruptly told, "Oh, no. We have not looked at anything from you. It takes ten days just to go through security here."

I was very frustrated with what appeared to be a lack of concern for pilots by the FAA. We have to do everything in exactly the scheduled time frame, but they are never in a hurry. Without a medical okay, I could not fly by myself.

Being frustrated with the FAA wasn't going to do me any good, so I asked two friends who were flight instructors to fly with me. This, I hoped, would get me enough practice so that when I finally flew again by myself, I would be safe and comfortable. I was used to flying several hours a week, so not flying for nine months really affected my confidence. On my first flight with Matt, instead of landing smoothly, I flared (leveled out) too high and bounced onto the runway. It was not normal for me to land like that, and I was quite humbled by the experience.

During this period of time without a medical release, I could not do any check-rides as an FAA Designated Examiner, so I lost that business to another designee. When I finally received my medical approval in the mail from the FAA, I worked at increasing my customers. I never did get enough to satisfy the FAA, since other designees were doing three times what I did. I also became rusty at doing them, so that was the end of that career.

I never expected that to happen as soon as it did, just as I had never expected to feel I was getting older. In my head, I was fit as a fiddle, but age was creeping up on me at 71.

CAMPING UNDER THE WING

During the summer, I was busy at the seaplane base and never traveled anywhere. When pilots returned from the biggest airshow in the world, the Experimental Aircraft Association's AirVenture in Oshkosh, Wisconsin, I listened to see what I was missing.

Some of the stories were about how massive the show was. They were exhausted from walking around and trying to see everything. There were over 10,000 airplanes of every make and model spread out between three airports — Fond du Lac (FLD) to the south, Appleton (ATW) to the north and the biggest with the largest number of planes, Wittman Regional Airport (OSH) in Oshkosh.

Other pilots told stories of flooding rainstorms and excessive heat. Nothing about attending appealed to me and I never thought I was missing anything. I stayed perfectly content at home teaching pilots how to fly seaplanes.

In 2016 while waiting to hear from the FAA that I was cleared to fly alone again, I was invited as a passenger to attend AirVenture by my pilot friend Linda Cioffi from Albany, N.Y. I never said no to an adventure, so I thanked her and we made plans of where to meet and what to bring. She was nice enough to fly east to the Auburn Lewiston Airport, spend the night, and we started our journey west from there.

She decided to fly in to the Fond du Lac airport as it was not as busy as the Oshkosh airport, and we took a shuttle each day to Oshkosh from there.

Flying from Maine to Wisconsin was uneventful. We were able to make the trip in one day as she flies a Cessna 182 that is fast enough to do that 800 nautical mile trip that quickly.

There were many aerobatic air shows during the day that were fun to watch, but we missed all the night shows. We left the field with some of her friends in the late afternoon after walking around all day. We enjoyed dinner with them, and they dropped us off at the Fond du Lac airport where we were to spend the night in our respective tents. Linda's tent was under one wing of her plane and mine was under the other as we happily crawled in for the night. Well, she happily did. I just about took the tent down when crawling in.

I then struggled to get undressed and into my PJs while lying down and then struggled to get dressed in the morning. When I crawled out of the tent, I would get tangled up again. I noticed a huge tent under another plane's wing that was big enough to move around and stand up in. I was thoroughly convinced to buy a bigger tent and never try the two-man version again. Ever.

In 2017 and flying again, I decided to fly to Oshkosh by myself in my Super Cruiser for three reasons: I wanted to camp under the wing of my airplane, be able to go back and rest in the afternoon and be amidst all the excitement. I did take a nap every day and happily climbed into my sleeping bag at 8 pm, missing all the night shows.

But before I could leave on my next adventure, I needed to talk to a mechanic. On a previous day, when starting the plane, I didn't have any trouble, but on the second start after fueling, the plane would not start as quickly as it normally did. I didn't want to run into any problems while traveling. The mechanic, Sean, said he would look and see what he could find. He carefully removed the cowl cover and looked at the engine. During his inspection he found a wire that was loose, causing the problem, and secured it. I was then on my way. He said it was a temporary fix and that he needed to do more to correct the problem when I got back, but I was safe to fly and shouldn't have any problem starting the plane after fueling along the way. He was right — I had no trouble at all.

I took off and settled into my peaceful role of flying and excited to be going on an adventure. Getting "flight following" is sensible when flying long distances and over mountains, so I called Portland ATC (Air Traffic Control) and reported my registration number, type of airplane, altitude, and destination. While I was climbing to a higher altitude to clear the mountains, Portland turned me over to Boston Approach.

"Good morning, Boston. Super Cruiser N4433M checking in 4,500' climbing 8,500' destination Syracuse SYR (Sierra Yankee Romeo).

Boston replied, "4433M. Are you on amphibious floats this year?" This is highly unusual for any casual conversation to be carried on and he took me by surprise. The thought was running through my head as to how on earth he knew me and that I flew on floats. The Boston departure station is in Nashua, N.H., and I didn't know anyone there. However, I loved being recognized.

"Yes I am." I didn't expect anything further, because Boston controllers are very busy with airline traffic coming and going.

He continued, "Didn't you fly scenic flights in Naples a few years ago?"

"Yes, I did."

"Where are you off to today?" He asked.

"I'm on my way to Oshkosh."

"I'm jealous." After what seemed like a long pause, "Are you married?" This floored me! I just laughed, said yes and continued on my way, thrilled to have such an experience.

"Well, safe flying," and that was the highlight of my flight. I sailed on from there. I've thought of many responses that would have been fun to say. My favorite was, "I can easily divert to pick you up. What time do you get out of work?" Unfortunately, I didn't think of that at the time.

After landing in Syracuse for fuel, I realized there were instrument conditions along my route from there. I was tired and decided to spend the night and continue to Oshkosh the following day. The entire trip was to take 10 hours in my plane, and I chose to spread those out over two days. It took four hours to get to Syracuse and then it would take six hours to Oshkosh. The next flight was to be broken up by a fuel stop at the St Clair County Airport in Port Huron, Michigan.

But then I diverted to an airport on the southeast end of Lake Michigan to avoid thunderstorms over Lake Michigan. I met three people that night at the airport where I landed who also decided to stay overnight. They flew in an Avenger that fascinated me. The wings fold up on the World War II-era torpedo bomber, which allowed more planes to fit on a flight deck during the war. In that condition, we were able to safely tuck all of our planes in the airport's hangar to keep them from the additional nasty looking storms we could see on radar coming our way from the west. Many other pilots flying in fast planes scurried about fueling and left to avoid the weather. They continued to Oshkosh. I was just too tired and had no intention of trying to outrun a thunderstorm over Lake Michigan in a slow airplane. I was quite content to stay right where I was to fly another day.

The pilot and his friends in the Avenger and I enjoyed dinner together, and I dropped them off at their hotel, assuring them I would pick them up in the morning. The Avenger is a faster plane and landed at Oshkosh the following morning prior to my arrival. Jason, a pilot friend from Portland who drove to Oshkosh with his two children, arrived before me as well. All six of these enthusiastic friends were waving to me on the side of the runway after I landed at the big show.

I was so excited to see people I knew and so happy to be on the ground, I was hanging out my open door smiling from ear to ear and waving back! Being greeted was an unexpected, pleasant surprise and started a weeklong experience I will never forget.

I was directed in an orderly fashion by men and women in volunteer's orange vests to follow along a rough grass taxiway. I was then escorted by people on scooters to my parking spot. As soon as I finished the long taxi, several men came over to help me push the plane back into place. One asked if I was going to enter my plane into competition, and I explained that no, I just want to be able to camp under the wing.

"Well you are now," he stated as he typed something into his cell phone. "When you register for camping, you give them the rest of the details on your plane."

Before I could follow his directions to sign in, two other young pilots came over to see if they could be of help. They happily took my camping equipment as I handed it to them out of the back of the plane. Another tall man with an orange vest pulled up in a four-wheeler and asked if he could help. Everything was piled into the back of that little green four-wheeler. I was told I couldn't put my tent up under the wing there while parked next to the runway. When I arrived, the field was full and they had put me outside the normal parking area for planes, but no tents were allowed that close to the runway. That was a restricted area due to the proximity to the runway during the airshows.

The two pilots who came over to look at the plane and help me with my gear said, "Mary, why don't you put your tent under our wing?" Normally my response would have been, "Oh that's okay. I'll find a spot." But instead, I said, "Thank you very much. I would really appreciate that." The four-wheeler slowly moved behind us as we walked down the row to their Cessna 172 in row 131.

I would like to say these two very nice young men helped me, but they took the responsibility of putting my tent together. The lovely new red six-person tent was unfortunately defective. It took at least 30 minutes to get the support rods into the channel on the top of the tent. Using some shampoo on their fingers, they massaged the fabric while pushing the rod through that channel and managed to get the tent set up for me. I can't imagine what that would have been like for me to do by myself. I didn't know about the soap trick. These two young men were B-52 pilots in the military, and I was so grateful they took the time to help me.

Everyone seemed fascinated with my plane and the fact that I flew all the way from Maine by myself. The way I was treated made me feel like royalty.

What happened to that attitude of "I can do this by myself?" Perhaps I feel more confident now, and I don't need to prove anything to anyone. I also found that when I allow people to help, they genuinely want to. I'm fascinated at how long it takes me to learn these life lessons.

After my B-52 pilot friends got me situated, some friends of theirs called to say they had a plane depart next to them and my hosts could move their plane down from row 131 to 91.

"Mary, why don't you move your plane over here in our spot? That way, you will be able to camp under the wing of your plane," one of them suggested.

I was exhausted from all the stressful emotions of flying three days to this event. I flew in the clouds most of the way without an autopilot, which normally isn't an issue, but add turbulence to the mix, and I had to work hard the whole flight to stay at altitude and on course. I decided I would move my Super Cruiser in the morning.

Camping under someone else's plane was a gift. There was a strong sense of freedom and camaraderie here with thousands of fellow pilots enjoying staying on the field. It wasn't about saving money by not staying in a hotel but being right in the middle of all the activity. It was exhilarating.

I moved my plane in the morning. As soon as I finished securing the plane in the warm sunshine with the right wing over my oversized red tent that I could stand up in, a golf cart pulled up right in front of me. A pleasant looking mustached man with an official looking badge pinned to his straw hat was the driver and a lovely woman, who I assumed was his wife, sat beside him. She wore a broad brimmed colorful ribbon on her white hat. There was a tall young man who I was introduced to as Jesse. He looked to be about 16 or 17.

The driver, Ray Johnson, introduced himself and his wife, Judy, while admiring my plane. He asked if I would be willing to taxi it to the other end of the field and into the "Vintage in Review" area. Evidently one of the first men who helped push my plane into place near the runway the day before texted Ray to come and see the plane.

With Jesse's help, we untied all the ropes, put them in one of the float compartments for storage, and with my invitation, he hopped right in the back of my tandem seating plane. We taxied for several long and bumpy moments on the uneven grass taxiway escorted by more volunteers on scooters with their orange vests. That was the start of day two. All this attention was something I never expected.

The Vintage in Review area had a small group of bleachers where interested people could hear all about the vintage planes. Each day, Ray had organized several different programs. My first day there was "Ladies Love Taildraggers" and there were three other planes already in position facing the bleachers. My plane, turned in the other direction and situated in the front corner, was facing the main thoroughfare. Here it immediately started catching the attention of people passing by. People started to gather around 4433M fascinated with the beautifully designed paint scheme with matching amphibious floats. The plane was white with a broad striking dark blue stripe running down the fuselage.

Curious spectators asked questions about the different ways to land on water and runways. I have spent many years as a seaplane instructor, so responding to their curiosity was easy and fun. The following day the other planes were moved back to their parking spots on the field, but my plane was kept there all week. I happily answered questions for several days.

People were sure that I only flew in light winds. I explained that if I needed to get somewhere, 35 knots was my limit. I went on to talk about how windless conditions result in "glassy water," which creates a dangerous situation due to the lack of depth perception. I have experienced coming in to land and at 50 feet above the water looked down and all I could see was the reflection of clouds. I then set up a 100-foot-a-minute rate of descent and touched down smoothly. If I didn't do that, there was a possibility of flying right into the water and getting overturned. When teaching pilots how to fly seaplanes, they didn't believe me until they experienced that condition themselves. They were always surprised to land unexpectedly.

There were tie-down ropes hanging from the underside of the wings and they asked about those. I explained that when standing on a ramp, or in the water at the beach, it was impossible to reach the tie-down ring, so the ropes facilitate the process of securing the plane. The ropes also help handling the plane from a dock.

With a wide smile, I also told them I did the splicing on those ropes. They were fascinated I could do that. Splicing makes a small loop for a handle. Done properly, it looks like it came finished from the manufacturer. The end, neatly pulled back into the main part of the rope, disappears. The splicing is one of the few things I can take credit for on this beautiful plane.

Several pilots asked if I had someone come from home to help me on the flight. That thought hadn't even crossed my mind. Did I look like I couldn't manage on my own? It must be the gray hair.

Later that night I realized this trip was the first time in my life I had gone somewhere because I wanted to go and didn't bring anyone else along. My, I was getting more independent and really enjoying life!

This trip made up for the nine months of not being able to fly after heart surgery. Flying by myself for three days and some of that time in instrument conditions demonstrated to me I really was capable and felt confident once again in my skills.

As people were asking questions and taking pictures on Friday, an official came along and put a sign on my propeller: AWARD WINNING PLANE. I was shocked. More people came to take pictures when they saw that sign and I had to back up. I was overwhelmed with all the attention I received that week and then to win a prestigious prize was totally unexpected. I had gone to Oshkosh to watch all the activities and camp under my wing. I never expected to win anything. The award said "AirVenture Oshkosh 2017, CLASSIC AIRCRAFT, OUTSTANDING CUSTOM CLASS C (151-235 HP) Mary Build, 1947 Piper PA-12 N4433M."

The next thing that happened was a woman came up to me and asked if she could interview me. Her name was Sparky, the same name my brothers gave me as a child. We spent about an hour together and have become fast friends. During the following months, Sparky called several times to confirm information and did a terrific job telling my story, along with the 1947 Super Cruiser's.

I was asked to go on a photo flight and asked Jesse, my willing helper since I arrived, to join me. He had never been in a seaplane other than the bumpy taxi trip to the "Vintage in Review" and was thrilled to go. On a previous day, as we walked around the grounds, Jesse had all the answers if I wanted to know anything about a plane I was not familiar with. It was a pleasure being with such an enthusiastic young man. Jesse has now finished college and flying for an airline.

Sparky's story about me was in the March 2018 issue of EAA Sport Aviation magazine along with several aerial photos. My daughter Lisa took several of the pictures at home that Sparky requested for the story. It was the first and only time in my life I was a centerfold!

N4433M at Oshkosh

TWIN EAGLES FIELD 71ME, NAPLES, MAINE

In August of 2000, I turned over the scenic flight business on Long Lake to another pilot, Jacki Rogers. She was a flight instructor who learned to fly when she was a kid and was very interested in taking over that business. She came along at just the right time.

I'd just sat down outside of the dilapidated office at Twitchell's Airport when Jacki came around the corner.

"Mary, if you ever decide to give up flying scenic flights on the causeway, I would be interested in talking to you about taking over that operation."

"Jacki, it just so happens I've been thinking of doing just that."

We set up a time to sit down and discuss the transfer of the lease. It was that simple to give up something that I loved, but I was ready to move on to my next undertaking. During my time in aviation, the next opportunity always presented itself at just the right time.

I wanted to start a good-quality seaplane flight school and to further develop my charter business. I had started the Naples Seaplane Service Corporation in 1997, so I kept that name for the flight school.

I came to the conclusion about starting my own seaplane base during the time I was a flight instructor in Florida in 1999. Becoming an FAA Designated Pilot Examiner was another goal, but I needed more hours teaching instrument students to qualify for that position. It's difficult to get many instrument students during the winter in Maine due to the weather, so I drove to Florida, found an apartment, and lived there for the winter working at the Orlando Executive Airport.

With too much free time when not at work, I was bored and had too much time to think.

I wanted to know what my path in life was, so I walked to a local bookstore looking for inspiration. I was not sure how I thought a book would do that, but I had faith.

As I walked the aisles in the bookstore, I couldn't find anything that resembled help in any way. What was the next road to take? After walking around the store several times, I finally gave up and picked up a novel, thinking it would keep me occupied. I wouldn't have the answers I wanted, but it would do.

Just after picking that book up, I walked around the corner and on the back side of the stand the novel was on, I found a workbook that reminded me of *What Color Is Your Parachute?*, which I had worked on years ago and which gave me the direction I needed at the time. I put the novel back in its place, bought the new workbook, and felt inspired.

I can't remember the name of it now...something similar to "Be Who You Are," which is just what I was looking for. I brought it back to the apartment and dug right in. I was excited about the possibility of having more to look forward to in my life. After answering all the questions, the suggestion was that I start a seaplane flight school.

I didn't own any property and couldn't imagine how I could accomplish such a goal. At the time, I thought I needed a land operation along with a seaplane base, just like Twitchell's Airport in Turner, where people could land on wheels on the runway or floats in the water.

I talked about my newfound dream with my friend Jim when I got home in the spring. He had lost his wife to cancer the previous year and spent a lot of time with me as a mentor. I wasn't looking for anything, I was simply telling him what I'd discovered about myself. He continued to work on a project and didn't respond one way or another to my comment. He wasn't much for conversation unless he was telling one of his aviation stories. Over the next 20 years, I realized that was just the way he took in information. He needed time to process and decide, in any given situation, what he would do...if anything.

When I gave up the scenic flight lease on Long Lake, I was recently divorced and living alone in a house Jim made available for me on Brandy Pond, just south of Long Lake.

The little brick house was poorly built, with no heat, but did have a fireplace in the living room and bedroom. I didn't need heat during the summer anyway, so that wasn't an issue. It was just temporary housing for me and very much appreciated. I could walk the quarter mile to my scenic flight operation where I worked that summer prior to Jacki's taking it over.

Walking peacefully home at night was the perfect way to end a busy day flying passengers. The house, sitting comfortably back from the pond, faced the early morning sunrise and the full moon when it arrived. It was a perfect spot for me. What a pleasant way to start the day with the sunrise and end the day with the moon shining off the water.

Jim started the habit of dropping in with two cups of coffee before I went to work, and we sat in the front yard enjoying the warmth of the early morning sun. We were discussing the start of the first hangar he had in mind when Stefen Lind walked into the yard. This tall blond young man casually greeted us with his usual air of confidence.

I couldn't believe my eyes. Stefen had worked as a waiter in the restaurant right next to the dock where I operated my scenic flights. He had moved to Oregon the year before. The thought of him coming back to live here again never entered my mind. Before he left for the west, he was my first student in a borrowed plane. I was terribly disappointed when he left, because he was making solid progress with his flying skills.

"What on earth are you doing here?" I asked.

"I've come to learn to fly."

"I thought you were taking lessons in Oregon and would have your private pilot's license by now."

"No," he said, "I couldn't find a teacher that I liked as much as you [building me up, for sure], so I've come back to finish my training here. What I really want is to learn on floats. I don't care anything about flying a land plane."

This sounded so familiar to me, as that was exactly how I thought when I wanted to fly when I was 30. Everyone told me I needed to start on land, but that wasn't true. I was excited to start one of my students as a seaplane pilot.

"I'll be happy to teach you on floats."

"However, I need a job to pay for the lessons and wonder if I could work for you?"

I didn't have any work that needed to be done, but I would find something.

"Okay," I said, "for every day you work, I'll give you an hour of flight training."

"Perfect. When can we start?"

"I'm available this afternoon and would love to get started."

Jim wasn't happy about having anyone else around. He was quite fond of working on his own.

"I'll keep him busy, so don't worry," I told Jim.

Trimming the bushes along the water was my initial thought to keep Stefen busy and out of Jim's way. That lasted about a week and then Jim found work for him clearing land for a new hangar. Jim got work done on the hangar, and I did the flight training. I was interested in having a hangar, so that arrangement worked just fine for me.

Stefen was my only student that year, so I was able to spend good quality time with him.

After working for us for four years doing whatever needed to be done, and getting all the training I could give him, Stefen left for Alaska with a commercial pilot's license with an instructor's certificate under his belt. His job in Alaska was flying scenic flights in Ketchikan. That is a difficult job in poor weather conditions, but he was capable. He came to me to be a seaplane pilot, and I gave him all I had to give so he could go on and become even more experienced than I. Flying in Ketchikan was not a job I would ever venture into.

In the early years of operating the Brandy Pond base, we couldn't land in the field in front of the hangars. There were power lines running diagonally across the field prohibiting any takeoff or landing operations. But we realized that if we could take off and land in the field, we could keep our planes at home and use them year-round. While Stefen was still with us, we decided that was something we wanted to do. He and Jim dug a two-foot-deep, 50-foot-long trench for those wires. We then had the power company lower and bury the wires underground.

We measured the field by walking it from the four-foot bushes at the water's edge to the neighbor's property and estimated the length to be 1,000 feet. I wanted to make sure we were operating legally, so I filed the paperwork with the FAA for approval.

With many FAA inspectors keeping an eye on my charter business over the years, I always learned something new when I flew with them, and, hopefully, I was able to pass along good seaplane piloting skills to them.

One of my inspectors, Dennis Delo, arrived at the Brandy Pond base, and we inspected the "landing strip" together. Inwardly, I did not think it possible approval would be granted, but he said, "I'll do the paperwork when I get back to the office."

I said, "This is a satisfactory strip?" Obviously it was if he just approved it, but I was very surprised.

His response: "I've seen worse."

That wasn't terribly encouraging, but if he said it was okay, I was okay. Coming from a former inspector in Alaska, I took his word for it.

He gave the field the designation of 71ME, and it was put on the aviation chart. Years later, using Google Earth to measure the field, I discovered it was only 800 feet—very short for a landing strip.

At the easterly end of the field, next to the water's edge, was a ramp going down into the water. We used that ramp for putting the seaplanes in and out of the water during the seaplane season of May to the end of October. It was just like a boat ramp.

Coming straight in over the water and landing to the west was the only way to approach the strip, while flying east over the water was the only way out. The trees towered over the 18-foot power lines at the western end and were too high to make a safe departure in that direction.

The grass was always cut, but it had low spots in it, making it rough to walk on. It also had a slight curve to the left. The ditch in the middle was eliminated by putting in a culvert, but if you didn't stay in the middle of that part of the runway, you might end up in the ditch on either side. This was not like any other runway where I had ever landed.

Well then, I thought, we have a landing strip. We have an airport along with a seaplane base. I could fly home any time of year and put the plane under cover in a heated hangar. I was thrilled.

I usually landed on paved runways at airports. The shortest was 2,100 feet by 50 feet wide in Turner. That was more than enough room, but the illusion, when flying in over high trees at the beginning of that particular runway, made the runway look much shorter.

I waited for Jim to land in our field so I could learn from his experience. He managed to be too busy, not interested, or waiting to see if I would go first. With no example to go by, I decided to figure it out myself.

I thought I had better find out just how short I could land first. I would have to fly over the four-foot-high bushes along the edge of the water at the beginning of the runway. Those bushes could not be taken down due to environmental regulations, which made the approach more challenging.

The best-case scenario would be to have a level approach and land right in the beginning of the runway. This field was not a place I wanted to find out if I could land short enough, so I practiced at the Auburn/Lewiston Airport, landing on the grass beside the runway and pretending there were bushes at the beginning of my touchdown spot.

I wasn't satisfied with the distance I covered after landing and rolling out the first time. I stopped within 1,000 feet, but that wasn't good enough. The second one was better, and the third approach and landing even better, when I landed and stopped in 500 feet. I was quite satisfied with that accomplishment and was ready to land at the seaplane base.

I circled the field twice, taking a good look from the air, trying to decide if I had overestimated my ability. I set up the approach using a nice slow airspeed of 55 mph and descended at my normal 500 feet a minute. Everything was fine on the approach until I came over those bushes and between very tall trees on either side, experiencing just how fast I was going. I never had that sensation at an airport, where there is almost always lots of room on either side of a runway.

I thought, Oh no! I'm going way too fast! I checked the airspeed indicator in the plane, and I was going as slow as I could, but my head was telling me something different.

I hope I'm doing the right thing trying this out before anyone else, I thought.

I stopped in half the distance of the field, turned the plane around, and taxied back to the hangar. My knees were shaking so badly, I could barely stand up. Much to my surprise, my knees shook every time I flew in there for the following two years.

I had one adventure after another landing in that field. If I didn't land and stop soon enough, I had the potential of taking off the clothes hanging on the line at the neighbor's house, and I really didn't want to do that. I never did disturb those overalls and denim shirts, but I must say I came close several times, especially when I was on skis. Brakes don't work at all in the snow. When the snow was deep, there was plenty of drag to slow me down, but when it was packed down, the slowing down process was sketchy.

In addition to the landing, the decision to go around (a term used for an aborted landing) needed to be made right in front of the hangar at the beginning of the runway. After that spot over the runway, the plane didn't have the capability of making it over the trees that towered over the power lines at the far end.

This strip was a one-way-in and one-way-out—unless it was very windy. Then it was possible to approach in the other direction over town, clear the trees, and land into the wind. When it's very windy, the plane travels in the air at the same speed, but the speed over the ground is reduced by the same amount. So, if my airspeed was 55 mph and the wind was blowing at 20 mph, my speed over the ground on an approach was 35 mph. The slow speed makes it possible to get over those trees and land in half the distance of the field and stop quickly.

There was only one time I couldn't land. The wind was five mph from the southeast, giving me a tailwind, but not enough wind to slow me down enough to come in over the trees and land in the other direction. I flew to the Fryeburg Airport, left the plane tied down on the ramp, and someone came over to pick me up. When the wind was more favorable another day, I was brought back to the airport, flew back, and landed in the field...knees still shaking.

Naples Seaplane Office

FLYING WITH JACKI

Jacki Rogers, the woman who took over the scenic flight operation from me on Long Lake, was enjoying her time flying passengers. She wanted to have another plane she could fly during the off season, so she purchased a Cessna 170B. That white and light-blue plane was pristine. She spent a lot of time trying to get used to handling that beauty, but with different characteristics than she was accustomed to, she was having trouble. She's a private person, so she never shared that information with me.

One day she called and said, "Mary, I need help."

I couldn't imagine why she needed my help. I thought she flew quite well.

"Jacki, I don't have any time in a 170."

Silence was her response. I didn't know her very well and thought she must be disgusted with my lack of willingness to help. I was a flight instructor, and I guess she thought I could.

A week went by and she called again. "Mary, I need help." That didn't give me very much information.

"Jacki, I'm sorry, but I don't have any time in a 170B and don't know the characteristics of that model." Silence again. Then I thought she was mad at me.

Another week went by and she said, "Mary, I need you to help me. I'm scaring myself." She was a woman with few words when she was upset, so I had to simply accept that she needed my help—period.

I finally went to Jim and asked, "Jim, what do I need to know about flying that plane? Jacki seems to think I can help her."

"After you land," he said, "pull back on that yoke and keep it there until the plane comes to a stop. That way, it won't bounce back and get any lift under the wings."

If that's all I needed to know, I could make sure she did that. Most accidents happen when losing control taking off and landing, especially in a tailwheel plane, so he must have assumed she was having trouble landing.

More modern planes have a nose wheel, making the takeoff and landing operations a little more stable. The tailwheel plane has a center of gravity behind the front wheels, creating the possibility of losing control on the ground more prominent.

So far, she hadn't crashed, so I called her back.

"Jacki, I'm willing to give you flight instruction as long as you're aware of my lack of familiarity. When would you like to get started?"

"How soon can you get here?"

I drove from Naples to the Limington Airport, where her plane was tucked away in the hangar. I was impressed with the care she was taking of this beauty. The interior was new, with special pockets she had made for pens, pads of paper, and sunglasses. Perfect. The plane looked innocent enough to me, and I couldn't imagine what she was having trouble with.

"So, what are you having trouble with?" I asked.

"You'll see," was her response. Few words again.

The first thing I noticed when I climbed into the copilot's seat was the amount of visibility in front. In most planes, I like to have the seat adjusted in a high enough position to see clearly, but no adjustments were necessary in this one.

When we took off, the attitude of the nose sloping down gave an illusion of not climbing. In other planes, the nose clearly comes up when you take off and climb. The takeoff went just fine, and Jacki seemed more comfortable than I. What on earth could she possibly need from me? We both flew many planes on a regular basis...land and sea.

She climbed up to 3,500 feet, which is a normal altitude for us to practice maneuvers. We always make sure to have enough room to get out of any unexpected, unusual attitudes.

"Now, wait till you see this. I'm having a terrible time just doing steep turns," she said.

This is a procedure practiced as a student pilot to develop the skill of dividing attention between the 45-degree bank angle, staying within 100 feet of the starting altitude, and beginning and ending at the same compass heading prior to turning in the opposite direction and repeating the turn in the other direction. As commercial pilots, we needed to be precise and not deviate to that 100-foot limit.

We had to keep our attention outside the plane instead of looking at the instruments that would make it easier to be accurate. The attitude indicator in the plane shows the artificial horizon, angle of bank, and whether you're climbing or descending. It's approximately three inches round with a line going through the middle simulating the horizon. There is a smaller thick line with a little dot in the middle indicating the airplane. At the top half of the circle are tick marks indicating the degree of bank the plane is turning. Using this indicator in instrument conditions is necessary for a pilot to see where the plane is in relation to the horizon, but in visual conditions, the outside world is the reference used for the attitude of the plane.

She started her first turn to the left and immediately dropped 150 feet, corrected, and climbed 200 feet over her intended 3,500 feet.

"Oh my," was my comment without even knowing I said it. Jacki was as skilled a pilot as I knew, and I couldn't imagine why she was having so much trouble maintaining altitude.

"Oh my," I said again when she turned to the right, and I think I added another, "Oh my," before she finished. She made it look like she had never flown those steep turns before.

"That's what I need help with," she said, exasperated.

"Well, let me give it a try to see what you're experiencing."

I was sure this was going to be an easy fix. Since I had never been in this model plane before, I wanted to handle the controls to see what she was dealing with. I started the 45-degree bank to the left and up I went, down and then up again.

"Oh my," said Jacki each time. I think she actually said, "Oh my," more times than I had when she was flying.

"Jacki, we have work to do." That was putting it mildly.

What was different than any other plane either of us had flown was that sloping nose. It was great for visibility on the ground, but the normal reference we used to the horizon to keep us at the same altitude was just not there.

Jacki and I flew for hours each day and found the reference point we needed to the horizon to stay level when doing steep turns. We both became more proficient as time went on.

One day, we flew over to Naples to check out the seaplane base for a little diversion from our work. Jacki was really good at short-field operations, so in the back of my mind, I thought she might want to land in there and have a cup of coffee. Jim's truck was in the middle of the runway, preventing us from landing. When Jim heard us overhead, he ran out and moved the truck. He jumped out and waved his arms indicating to come in.

"He wants us to land in there," I said.

"No way am I going to attempt that," she said as we circled the field.

Jim continued to frantically wave his arms.

"You can do this, Jacki."

"You do it."

"No. This is your plane, you do it," I said.

We continued to fly around the field taking a good look, and I said again as we rounded the far end of the field, "You can do this, Jacki." Jim was still out there encouraging us to land.

"You do it, Mary."

I had no intentions of flying her plane in there. Taking the challenge with my plane was one thing, but I didn't want to do that in hers.

"Jacki, landing in there is really fun. You should give it a try."

"You do it."

"No, thanks."

As we came around the second time, right where we would usually set up for the landing, I said, "Okay. I'll do it." I just couldn't give up that challenge.

I took over the controls from my seat. Everything was set up in the plane, and I flew at our normal slow landing speed of 50 knots, which is about 58 mph. This model has 40 degrees of flaps, making it capable of flying at very slow approach speeds. With the sloping nose, I could clearly see my whole landing area. I landed right in front of the hangar, stopped in half the distance of the field, and smiled. What a feeling of satisfaction!

Jacki and I tell this story every time other pilots ask if we fly together.

Jacki went on to land there several times. When she got out of the plane, she looked calm, as if it was something she did all the time. Years later, I found out her knees shook just like mine did, but neither of us wanted to admit that to anyone.

Another time, she and I were practicing takeoffs and landings in my plane on wheels. I picked her up in Limington, and we flew around for over an hour having a great time getting more proficient. Jacki is also a flight instructor, so when either of us needed supervision, we helped each other.

We were at the Oxford Airport taking turns taking off and landing when I realized it was getting late in the day. We were running out of daylight. It was just before Christmas when the sun sets around four p.m. here in Maine. Flying 25 miles from Oxford to Limington, and then back 12 miles to Twin Eagles field would put me at a risk of trying to land in our field in the dark. I had just learned how to land there in daylight and couldn't risk even thinking about landing in the dark.

"Jacki, would you mind coming with me back to my field and I'll drive you home?"

"No, I'm fine with that," she said.

I flew around the field, which looked inviting with a light dusting of snow covering the grass. The first part of my landing went just fine, but during rollout, I broke through a thin layer of snow-covered ice that was hiding a mud puddle. Mud splashed up, covering my windscreen and making it difficult to see where I was going. There was plenty of room, so that wasn't a concern. I taxied back, got out in front of the hangar and realized my poor, beautiful white Super Cruiser was covered with dark-brown partially frozen mud that was dripping off the fuselage and wings. What a mess.

"Come on, Jacki, let's get this off as fast as we can so it doesn't stain the white fabric." More modern planes are metal now, but back in 1947 when this plane was built, fabric was used to cover it.

Jacki has never let me live that down. Cleaning off a muddy plane had nothing to do with flight training! It took us well over an hour with several buckets of clean, warm water in the hangar to get that mess cleaned up.

THE APPLE ORCHARD

I felt such joy being healthy after heart surgery and that I was allowed to fly again. While waiting for the FAA to finally decide I could fly by myself, I thought I would be okay if they decided against it. Being told I could never fly again would have been crushing. I wouldn't have been happy.

I heard others complain that it was too cold to fly or too much trouble in the winter. Shoveling 240 cubic feet of snow in front of the hangar is a lot to do after a long day shoveling at home. The cowl cover was heavy and awkward, and it needed to be put in the back of the plane in case I stopped somewhere. That cover was keeping the engine nice and warm while the engine heater was warming it up for flight. Shoveling and hassling with the cowl cover alone could be too much, but for me, it was all part of being able to fly in the winter and enjoy the pristine clear air and beautiful views.

I asked for help getting the plane out onto the ice-covered ramp and I climbed in. One leg refused to come in with me due to the multiple layers of clothing I had on in addition to my heavy winter boots. I dragged it in. I was not going to freeze if I got stuck somewhere and needed to be prepared.

My plane was equipped with wheel penetration skis, where the wheels protruded through the skis just enough to make it possible to roll the plane out of the hangar and then taxi to the runway to take off. As I took off and left the runway, I realized how freeing flying is. I was grateful every time I took off. I looked around to see where I could land and decided it wouldn't be safe because the snow was too deep. If I stopped, the front of the skis would go under the snow, and I didn't have my snowshoes with me to make my own runway to take off again. Trudging along in deep snow with snowshoes is hard work. I would have to pack down two rows for the airplane skis so I would be able to take off.

I then thought I didn't have to stop. Little Sebago Lake had many snowmobile tracks on otherwise untouched snow. Looking at the tracks,

I saw they were filled with snow and not water, telling me the ice was safe. I circled around as I descended, checking out the conditions on the lake, and found a nice long stretch where I could touch down and have plenty of room to take off again without stopping. As I was circling, all the people who were ice fishing waved to me, and I rocked my wings in our wonderful unspoken exchange.

I came back on the power and added flaps to be able to descend at a steeper grade, but not increase my speed. I was enjoying the little flutter of my happy heart. It was an adventure, and I loved every minute.

Right near the lake, I added some power, giving me lift to slow down my descent. I could barely feel the soft snow under my skis. I added power to scoot along on the surface to take in the thrill and then added more power to take off.

I just had to do that again. Enjoying the same sensation of soft powdery snow, this time I touched down next to my original tracks. Where's the next place I can land? I thought. I didn't think I would find anyplace else, but again, who said I had to stop and get stuck? Another lady pilot had a grass strip within a ten-minute flight, so I flew over and to see how that looked. Heavenly! It didn't have a track on it, and I had permission to land there anytime. I flew down and did another soft landing, tracked the runway a short distance, and took off again.

There was an apple orchard in Standish with another grass strip, so I went to check that out. Again, a perfect place to do another touch-and-go! I had never landed there before, and the approach between the woods and the orchard was just beautiful. Another soft run on the snow and I took off over the antique farmhouse at the end of the runway and returned to the ice-covered ramp just as happy as I could be.

I will never take my health for granted again and will continue to appreciate every time I can fly. When I look back on my life, I know how important flying is to my very existence. In fact, it may be the most important relationship I've ever had.

I was married three times, which I don't even like admitting because it makes me feel like a failure. I know I'm not. I could go on and on about how "he said this, and he said that," but the bottom line is that I made three poor choices. It was not that they were bad people, but they were not good for me. I chose men who were emotionally unavailable, had terrible tempers, and were on the rebound from recent losses or failed relationships. Anyone in their right mind would have seen the facts and waited. I didn't wait. Looking back, I realize I did learn important lessons from those relationships that have helped me tremendously.

In my first marriage to Tony, it became obvious that I needed help. I'd had enough of feeling inferior. I knew I had more to offer. I went for two scenic flights with my daughters during that marriage, which inspired me to become a seaplane pilot. I investigated the possibility but was not able to do so at the time. I knew Tony wouldn't support it, plus the timing just wasn't right with the girls being so little. The best thing to come out of that was I started to realize there were more challenges available for me, and I didn't doubt my ability to accomplish the goal of becoming a pilot.

In my second marriage, I started flying and received support at first that didn't last long. What he didn't realize is that I couldn't be talked out of flying—and I certainly couldn't be taken away from something that I credited with changing my life. I knew being a pilot was what I was meant to be. He had a negative attitude about my plans to buy a bigger plane that would help expand my business doing scenic flights. I lost respect for him because he tried to sabotage my progress, but I continued to fly.

In my third marriage, Jim was my mentor at first and then became my aviation idol. I wanted to be a great seaplane pilot just like he was. He shared his aviation experiences in a variety of ways. I listened carefully to learn from his adventures, as well as from his previous mistakes when flying. He never told me how to fly, but I watched carefully and learned. When he stopped flying due to his age and growing lack of interest in aviation, he didn't want to be around planes any longer and moved to Northern Maine—without me. I was still actively flying.

It wasn't a job. It wasn't a hobby. It was something that I was good at and that made me feel good about myself. I was out in the public dealing with people who respected what I was doing. It was something that I wanted to learn more about in every possible way. I wanted to listen to other pilots, read, study, and improve. It was the first time in my life that I found something that was perfect for me. I couldn't have that taken away, even if it meant ending another marriage.

When I was doing seaplane scenic flights, I was delighted when a woman came to see me the day after her flight. She thanked me for inspiring her to accomplish her goals. She said, "You've accomplished something out of the ordinary for a woman, and you obviously love what you do. After telling me your story of how you got into aviation, I know I can do the same thing. I don't want to become a pilot, but I've had a desire to do something different and have been afraid I would be criticized. Now I know I can do it, and it won't matter what other people think."

I don't know what that something was, but what I'm doing is not only good for me, but for others, too. I need to keep flying.

ACKNOWLEDGMENTS

I had a story to tell and needed help telling it in the most effective way. In the past, I had the privilege of working with Joan Hunter, a writing coach in Bridgton. When I contacted her about coaching me while writing my memoir, she suggested I work with a preestablished group of writers she had worked with for years.

At my first session with them, I firmly stated that I was not a writer. Marcel Moreau, a member of the group, quickly responded, "When you pick up a pen you become a writer." They were a collection of talented writers who had a remarkable way of expressing themselves in written words. Joan, as their coach, was famous for saying, "I want to hear more about that." So, I set out to do what I could. I was sure I couldn't match up to their fine work, but I had a story to tell, and they helped me say what I needed to say. I immediately felt a part of a caring group of people who encouraged me to continue through sometimes difficult memories. Once past those, I could continue with what I loved and what I've learned. If it was not good, or not of interest to them, they gently guided me. Guided me to explore my story and make it the way it should be.

I wanted to inspire, as I have been encouraged to do, but it's been more of a self-discovery process. My writing sometimes feels like a pendulum going from one mood to another: sometimes gently and sometimes abruptly transitioning from my childhood to the joy of flying that made me who I am today.

I had a sense of being on a team with my fellow writers. Everyone had different strengths. They were willing to put their all into the game. This is how we won in so many ways. We became friends, confidants, mentors, and critics all in one package. Everyone gave constructive criticism. How will I ever thank Marcel, Susan Gassett, Corinne Martin, Edy Netter, Bob Bittenbender, Margaret Jones, and Margi Huber for their caring contributions? A special thanks to Joan Hunter, who brought us all together. I'm a better person for knowing all of them.

When I finished editing my work using the suggestions from my writer's group, I sent individual chapters to Janice Wood, an experienced aviation editor. I can't imagine putting together this document without her help. Both her patience and efficient editing were extraordinary.

Many friends often asked if I had finished my book. Those questions often spurred me on to continue writing. I must say it is easier for me to fly a plane than it is to write, but I was encouraged by everyone to keep writing. They found merit in my story.

I gave my rough copy prior to printing to Meredith Edelman, a friend of over fifty years. She had some valuable suggestions that I readily accepted. She then gave me the best compliment by saying, "If my granddaughter ever gets to a point in life when she doesn't know what direction to go in, I will give her this book." Thank you, Meredith.

Then, my neighbor Cyndy Papken read it and made another suggestion that I accepted. Friends are invaluable, and I will be forever grateful for their comments.

When I thought I had a finished product that was ready to print, I sent it off to Maine Authors Publishing. The editors there made more corrections, making sure it *was* ready to print. Michelle Hodgdon put it all together like a piece of artwork that is now called a book. Thank you all for helping me keep my aviation experiences alive by writing about and sharing them.